T0385343

About the Author

Beth Kempton is a Japanologist, self-help author and writer mentor, whose books have been translated into more than twenty-five languages. Beth has been a student of Japanese life for quarter of a century, and has two degrees in Japanese.

Beth previously trained in TV presenter skills at NTV in Tokyo and, many moons ago, hosted her own TV show on Yamagata Cable Television. Over the years she has taken lessons in Japanese papermaking, flower arranging, pottery, *noren*-making, calligraphy and weaving. She is also a *Reiki* Master and a qualified yoga teacher.

Her work has been featured in a variety of publications including *TIME* magazine, British *Vogue*, *Wanderlust*, *Yoga* magazine, *Psychologies*, *Breathe*, *Vanity Fair*, the *Sunday Times*, the *Times Literary Supplement* and *Dezeen*.

Beth has long been a seeker of beauty, and as a writer she uses words to wrangle big questions about how to live well. As a mentor, Beth offers support and inspiration to writers and dreamers, teaching how words and ideas can heal, inspire, uplift, connect and help us make the most of our time in this beautiful world. Her company, Do What You Love, has delivered original online courses to over 100,000 people, helping them to navigate life, live creatively and do what they love.

Having lived and worked in Japan for many years, Beth now enjoys a slow-ish life by the sea in rural Devon, England, with her husband Mr K and their two young daughters.

dowhatyouloveforlife.com / bethkempton.com /
bethkempton.substack.com
Facebook/X @dowhatyoulovexx
Instagram @bethkempton

Also by Beth Kempton

BETH KEMPTON

KOKORO

JAPANESE WISDOM
FOR A LIFE WELL LIVED

PIATKUS

PIATKUS

First published in Great Britain in 2024 by Piatkus

7 9 10 8 6

A CIP catalogue record for this book
is available from the British Library.

ISBN 978-0-349-42558-0

Typeset in Bembo by M Rules
Printed and bound in Great Britain by
Clays Ltd, Elcograf S.p.A.

Papers used by Piatkus are from well-managed forests
and other responsible sources.

Piatkus
An imprint of
Little, Brown Book Group
Carmelite House
50 Victoria Embankment
London EC4Y 0DZ

The authorised representative
in the EEA is
Hachette Ireland
8 Castlecourt Centre
Dublin 15, D15 XTP3, Ireland
(email: info@hbgi.ie)

An Hachette UK Company
www.hachette.co.uk

www.littlebrown.co.uk

This book is dedicated to

my friend,
Lisa Moncrieff,
1981–2022

and

my mother,
Christine Nicholls,
1944–2023

I will carry you in my heart, always.

A Note on the Use of Japanese

In this book, the Hepburn system of romanisation is used for Japanese terms, including the names of people, with long vowels indicated by macrons. There are a few exceptions to this, including a number of place names that are commonly written with a particular spelling, such as Tokyo, Kyoto and Niigata. Foreign nouns that have become accepted into general English usage are shown in their accepted form without macrons, such as aikido instead of *aikidō* and noh instead of *nō*.

Japanese personal names have been written in standard English name order for ease of reference (first name followed by surname), except for historical figures most commonly known by a name given in the traditional Japanese name order (family name first).

When referencing people, the suffix -san is sometimes used as a term of politeness. Mountains can also be referred to as '-san' (such as 'Fujisan' for Mount Fuji), but in this case the suffix is a reading of the character for mountain. When the suffix –sensei is used, this refers to a teacher or professor. Rōshi after a name indicates a Zen teacher.

For effect, in naming the three parts of this book I have borrowed the literal translations of the Chinese characters used in the names of the three mountains of Dewa (Black Wing[1], Moon, Sacred Spring[2]), but in reality they are commonly known as Hagurosan, Gassan and Yudonosan respectively.

Please note that this book includes many references to the work of Zen Master Eihei Dōgen[3], who lived in thirteenth-century Japan. There is not sufficient room in a book like this to share his original teachings, which take up entire volumes of their own. Rather, I offer my personal response to those teachings, in the context of the questions raised in this book. If you want to experience his original texts and dive deeper into his ideas, please refer to the Bibliography.

Contents

羽黒山

Part One: Hagurosan

Encountering the present on Black Wing Mountain

月山

Part Two: Gassan

In the shadow of death on Moon Mountain

湯殿山

Part Three: Yudonosan

Rebirth on Sacred Spring Mountain

Contents

Foreword

by Professor Yoshinori Hiroi

In my early forties I had a strange experience on Yatsugatake, the volcanic mountain range stretching from Nagano to Yamanashi, in the heart of Japan's main island of Honshū. Home to flying squirrels, raccoon dogs, foxes and bears, the area's abundant flora and fauna have supported human life since prehistoric Jōmon times[1], evidenced by the remarkable artefacts found there dating back thousands of years.

I had visited the area many times. Living in Tokyo back then, I escaped to Yatsugatake anytime I needed to restore a sense of peace in my *kokoro*. But that particular day was different.

Standing quietly on the earth on Yatsugatake, I felt a sense of connection through time to the people who lived there ten thousand years ago, and all the people who have lived there since, live there now, and will live there in the future. With that sense of connection arose an understanding of the way life and death is viewed in Japanese culture, at three distinct levels.

On the surface is the modern material individual view, that when we die we are simply no more. On another level is the

Buddhist view, which has been around in Japan since the sixth century, and is a conceptual, abstract idea related to the universal. The third level is the original Shintō view, which is connected to nature in a very real way. This indigenous view holds that nature itself has insight, and is a fusion of being and not being. This is deeper than just the cycle of life, and expands to take in the origin of the world. It is related to energy, in us and in everything. It also reminds us that nature itself has a kind of spirituality.

This experience changed how I feel about dying, and consequently how I feel about living. I felt utterly liberated. My *kokoro* felt free.

Many aspects of Japanese culture are difficult to explain, but that does not mean it isn't worth the effort. I have spent many hours with Beth discussing life, death and the importance of the *kokoro*, and I know she will be a trusted guide by your side.

We are entering a time of transition, when our very existence depends on a shift from material growth to spiritual growth. Our approach to life has ramifications for the future of human society. It is essential that we think about how to live, individually and collectively, in order that we may make the most of our lives, and make choices which benefit humanity and nature far beyond our own existence.

Take care on this journey of a lifetime.

PROFESSOR YOSHINORI HIROI
Kyoto University Institute for the Future of Human Society
(formerly the Kokoro Research Centre)

Prologue

'Any dreams?' he asks, raising the blinds to take in the first shades of morning.

'Just the usual,' I say, pouring some tea.

But thinking about it, 'the usual' is not that usual at all, unless it's usual to have had a recurring dream since the age of forty, featuring a bald man dressed in robes so dark they must have been fashioned from the fabric of night. Unless it's usual for the man in that dream to be holding a sphere of intense golden light, illuminating only the moment in front of him, not the dark space behind. Unless it's usual to sense three shadowy figures at his back, and not know who they are, but not to be afraid.

I pick up my tea and drift towards my writing room. I light a candle, as I do at 5 a.m. most days. And I begin to write the story of the man, and the sphere of light. Of life and death and life again.

A story of discovering the heart's wisdom. A tale of unravelling time.

Introduction

When I was seventeen, Japan wrote me a letter. I couldn't read it at first, written as it was in one of the most complex and beautiful languages in the world. I stared at it for a long while, until the *kanji* characters began to swim off the page and swirl around me. They settled on my skin and then melted into it. Japan does that, you see. It arrives quietly and never leaves.

Nearly three decades ago, I packed my teenage bedroom and fat new dictionaries into a single suitcase, and left for a year. On the surface I was heading east to study the language, but there was something else. Deep down, I could sense a pull, the promise of an important secret hidden within the layers of Japanese life, perhaps.

When I had dropped the bombshell of an idea to ditch my well-thought-out career plan of an economics degree and accountancy for the chance of an adventure in a faraway land, instead of trying to dissuade me, my mother took me to a bookshop. We went to the travel section, which only had a handful of books about Japan. I picked up a travel guide and it fell open at a photograph of a pagoda covered in snow. Something inside me fizzed. Later, I stretched out on my bed and thumbed through every page. Here, an open fan lay alone on dark wooden floor, next to a raked sand garden. There, a small child posed in front of a wall of huge white *daikon* (winter radishes, the like of which I had never seen). On one page, a gently curving red bridge crossed a rushing river. On the facing page, a long line of moss-covered statues sat in a shady forest, waiting. There was talk of volcanoes, rice fields, tropical islands and remote shrines.

I had only ever been to France, on a school trip. Japan was a world I knew only in my imagination, and yet as I lay there poring over a photograph of two silhouetted figures sitting in quiet contemplation in a shadowy temple, looking out over a bright garden beyond, I sensed something that has never left me. A hidden truth about what it means to live well.

This pull towards Japan has been a siren call throughout my adult life. In answering that call I have been blessed by many encounters with people whose ways of seeing and being have influenced the way I live for the better.

It should have been no surprise, then, that when I hit midlife and sensed a rumbling beneath the surface of my highly organised days, I felt drawn to return.

Why *kokoro*?

When I began studying Japanese all those years ago, one of the first characters I learnt was 心 which is read *kokoro*, or in some situations, *shin*. I was drawn to its simplicity and how it seemed to brush itself onto the page, each inked stroke leading effortlessly to the next. Back then, I was taught the most basic of translations: 'heart'.

As a word, *kokoro* is highly visible in everyday life in Japan – it appears in calligraphy at temples, on posters, in adverts, in company names, in poetry and in daily conversation – and yet it alludes to something invisible and deeply personal. If you were to ask one hundred native speakers of Japanese to define it, you would get one hundred different answers.

Over the years, I had noticed that English-language versions of books about Zen, tea, Noh theatre and martial arts often rendered 心 not only as 'heart' but also as 'mind', 'heart-mind' or 'spirit', depending on the context. I found this both fascinating and confusing, because in my native English, 'heart', 'mind' and 'spirit' were very different things.

When I began to get overwhelmed by midlife and found myself carrying many burning questions, somehow I *knew* before I knew that *kokoro* was part of the answer.

Even now, after five years of researching, I hesitate to offer a definitive translation of *kokoro*, not least because the term is used in so many ways, but allow me an imperfect attempt for now.

The *kokoro* is the intelligent heart, which communicates our innate wisdom and responds to the world in the present moment, in the form of felt impulses. It is the source of our innate wisdom – the wisdom we carry deep within, which is untainted by societal pressure, expectation and other people's opinions. The *kokoro* can help us sensitively navigate relationships and choose a life path of ease and freedom through the moment-to-moment decisions we make each and every day.

The ability to recognise the wisdom of the *kokoro* is essential to an awakened, felt experience of the world. Through my midlife journey, I have come to understand twelve principles for a life well lived informed by the *kokoro*. Together, we will explore each of these in turn (one per chapter). In some cases we will explore the principle directly, in others it will be implicit in the stories that I share. I hope you will contemplate each one in the context of your own life, whatever life stage you are in, and let it guide you towards answers to your own questions.

TWELVE PRINCIPLES FOR A LIFE WELL LIVED, INSPIRED BY JAPANESE WISDOM

1. A life well lived is a life well examined.
2. A life well lived is a life experienced heart-mindfully.
3. A life well lived is a life enriched by stillness.
4. A life well lived is a life we are present to.
5. A life well lived is a life lived in full awareness of the impermanence of everything.
6. A life well lived is a life infused with the bittersweetness of love.
7. A life well lived is a series of mountains climbed.
8. A life well lived is a life of integrated layers.
9. A life well lived is a life fully expressed.
10. A life well lived is a life well nourished.
11. A life well lived is an unfolding path paved with what feels right.
12. A life well lived is an intentional life, lived fully and in gratitude.

How to use this book

Kokoro is structured in three parts inspired by three sacred mountains known collectively in Japanese as Dewa Sanzan, which can be found in Tōhoku, a remote and beautiful region of northern Japan:

- **In Part One, inspired by Hagurosan,** the mountain of the present and earthly desires, we take stock of where we are and consider what really matters at this point in our lives.
- **In Part Two, as we climb Gassan**, the mountain of death and the past, we face up to our own mortality and consider what death can teach us about living.
- **In Part Three, we encounter Yudonosan**, the mountain of rebirth and the future, where we contemplate how we want to live for the rest of our time on earth, however long we may have.

This trio of mountains forms the backbone of this book, but our travels will also take us beyond them to many lesser-known parts of the Japanese countryside, where we will encounter contemporary pioneers, the ghosts of ancestral thinkers and the spirits that inhabit the land. Collectively, they will show us why having a true sense of *kokoro* can transform our experience of the world, our relationships and our understanding of a life well lived.

The people we encounter along the way are from all walks of life, backgrounds and beliefs, but they all have one thing in common: they are highly attuned to the wisdom of their *kokoro*. In some cases, this manifests in the life path they are walking; in other cases, it informs the way they interact with others, or in their relationship to the natural world. In some, it shows up as a deep commitment to beauty in art and culture.

The wisdom found in these pages has drifted into my open hands like flower petals on a breeze, gathered conversation by conversation on my wanderings through Japan. In writing it down, I am gently blowing those petals in your direction. My intention with this book is to share what Japan and its culture

have so generously taught me, in case that can be a doorway
for you too.

In this book, you'll learn:

- Why these three sacred mountains hold the keys to
  choosing a new path anytime we like
- What a thirteenth-century Zen Master can teach us about
  the nature of time and why this changes everything
- What encountering death can teach us about living well
- How to tune in to and take care of your *kokoro*, and let it
  guide you daily as you cultivate a life well lived.

As such, this book is a guide for navigating life in general, and
times of transition in particular, but while it is a self-help book
of sorts, you won't find a series of life hacks and quick solutions
offered here, as if there were such a thing as a one-size-fits-all
answer to the questions that we carry. Instead, this is an invitation
to join me on a pilgrimage, away from the rush of daily life, to
seek out a new context for our questions, allowing clarity to arise
in its own good time.

One of the most difficult yet important things to grasp about
Japanese culture is that concepts and answers to questions are
often *aimai* (曖昧), which means vague. This is not because of a
lack of knowledge on the part of the speaker, but rather because
of a tendency towards harmony. Ambiguity is often seen as a
sign of respect. This cultural value is said to have arisen due to
the geographical nature of Japan, as an island nation covered in
mountains, where historically people have had to cooperate in
tight-knit communities in order to survive. Still today group
harmony is paramount, and this often spills over into a sense of
thoughtfulness in personal encounters.

I want to share with you my experience of Japan directly, which is why I have included certain conversations and descriptions of my interactions with the natural world. Some of the wisdom offered up by these encounters is implicit rather than explicit, as is often the way in Japan, so I encourage you to go slowly and let it soak in.

At the end of each chapter, you will find a set of three journaling questions to prompt your own inquiry. You might like to start a new journal for this purpose, so you can capture your thoughts as we travel together. When we get to the end and look back, you will be able to see how far you have come. I have called these questions '*Kokoro* Work' and I invite you to answer them without editing your words between brain and page. Write whatever wants to flow out, without judgement. Feel your way to the answers, and you will be amazed at what reveals itself when you let your *kokoro* lead the way.

(Note: if you are curious to learn more about the wide range of uses of the term *kokoro* in Japanese life and language, please refer to the 'Anatomy of the *kokoro*' appendix at the back of this book.)

A word on 'Japanese wisdom'

In Japan, many people practise more than one religion, usually a combination of Buddhism and the indigenous nature-based faith of Shintō. Personally, and certainly in this book, I do not advocate belief in any particular faith but, rather, am curious about how people live.

For the purposes of research, I have had conversations over tea, climbed mountains and meditated in various places across Japan with priests, nuns, monks, mountain ascetics, and lay followers of many different traditions and belief systems, including Sōtō

Zen, Rinzai Zen, Tendai Buddhism, Shingon Buddhism, Jōdo Buddhism, Shintō, Shugendō and Christianity, as well as with agnostics and atheists. These encounters have been too numerous to detail equally in the pages of this book, but my approach to life has been informed by all of them and I have tried to bring the most vital to the fore through the experiences I share here. These reflections, infused with the influence of the writings of Japanese historical figures, contribute to what I refer to in this book as 'Japanese wisdom'.

In addition, some of the 'Japanese wisdom' we will receive along the way is not from people at all but from the land and from nature – particularly from the mountains, which are believed to be the home of ancestral spirits. There is also an ancient belief that mystical powers can dwell in words themselves. *Kotodama* (言霊), literally 'word-spirits', give power to language when used ritually, and it is believed by many that these can influence us on a deep level. This has certainly been my experience, climbing mountains and chanting sacred words over and over during this journey, as you will discover.

Please note I have changed some details of the *yamabushi* train-ing I undertook in order to respect a thousand-year-old tradition of secret practice.

As you read, I encourage you to throw yourself fully into the adventure with me and sense the wisdom rising up from beneath your feet as we walk, in the space between us, and hidden between the lines of what is said by those we encounter. Perhaps between chapters you might enjoy spending some time in nature, reflecting on your own story and where you see it in mine. As we travel together we will receive gentle teachings that can guide us back to the original wisdom in our own *kokoro*.

Journey with me

To explore the *kokoro* is to explore the very essence of what it means to be human in this tough yet devastatingly beautiful world.

The path of this book traces the most difficult year I have known, as a series of unexpected events unfolded just as I passed the threshold of statistical midlife. This past year has taught me vital lessons about the fragility of life, and our lack of control in the great scheme of things, while reminding me to treasure what is precious and to trust in my own heart's wisdom.

As we move through the cycle of the seasons together, you will witness my reckoning, recalibration and renewal, and I hope you will draw inspiration from my experience to support your own life transitions.

*I used to think that the older I got the more I would
    know for sure.*
I was wrong.

*I used to think that by the time I was in midlife I'd have
    everything figured out.*
I was wrong.

*I used to think that if I never spoke of death it would not
    come near my door.*
I was wrong.

I used to think that hiding your emotions showed strength.
I was wrong.

I used to think that if we just held on tightly enough,
          things would last for ever.
I was wrong.

I used to be afraid of being wrong.
I am not afraid any more.

A life well lived begins and ends with the *kokoro*. May this book be exactly what you need right now, and may it long remain with you as you embrace all that is to come.

BETH KEMPTON
Kyoto, 2023

羽黒山

PART ONE: HAGUROSAN

Encountering the present on
Black Wing Mountain

Put your ear to the earth and you'll hear this mountain speak of gods and ghosts. Press your skin to the bark of this old tree and you'll learn of the strange shadow that once passed over this place and the cloaked man who ran behind it.

Tip your ear to the sky and you'll hear echoes of ancestral birdsong telling the story of a slain emperor, a fleeing prince and a mystical three-legged crow, a yatagarasu, *guiding him to safety. Follow the whispers of the wind and you'll discover that the tomb atop this mountain venerates that prince, who remained in this forest and gave his life to mountain worship, as the crow gave its name to the land.*

Come as a pilgrim, offer silence as you climb, and you might just hear a welcome.

'Yōkoso. I am Black Wing Mountain.'

As one of the three sacred mountains of Dewa Sanzan, Hagurosan (lit. 'Black Wing Mountain') is said to represent the present and earthly desires. People have journeyed to Hagurosan for centuries, often travelling hundreds of miles on foot, to pray for health and good fortune in this life. This is where our story begins.

CHAPTER 1

LIFE

The scroll unravels

I n a small thatched cottage on the south coast of England, I was ironing with one eye on a crumpled-up skirt and one eye on the funeral of Her Majesty Queen Elizabeth II, which was unfolding on the screen in my living room. Generally, I believe life is too short for ironing, but that day I found comfort in easing creases from cotton as the royal procession solemnly advanced towards Westminster Abbey.

Just as the State Trumpeters of the Household Cavalry sounded the Last Post, my husband's phone rang. He glanced down and took the call in the kitchen, while I stayed standing with our daughters for two minutes of silence, remembering a life lived in service.

The trumpets sounded again, and my husband called my name. The tone of his voice sent a dart into my heart and I knew. My friend Lisa had died, aged forty-one.

It wasn't until later that I realised something in me had died too that day: the part that believed that if you are a good person and work hard, fill in your planner and eat your vegetables, you'll be blessed with a long and happy life.

The unfairness of it all was pumping through my veins as I hauled myself up Hagurosan a few weeks later. Wearing boots laced with sorrow, I felt the weight of my friend's loss in every step, all the heavier knowing that Lisa, who loved Japan, would never make this journey.

Up ahead my guide climbed steadily. He was a man of the mountains, wearing a distinctive outfit with stiff sleeves and wide *hakama* trousers cinched in above the ankle. *Shiroshozoku*, the clothing of the dead. The heavy white cotton was rendered sky blue in places as shadows fell across him, cast by the late autumn sun.

His name was Master Hayasaka, and he was a *yamabushi* (lit. 'one who lies on the mountains'), a contemporary steward of the ancient indigenous faith of Shugendō. Roughly translating as 'the way of attaining divine natural powers through ascetic training'[1], Shugendō carries echoes of Shintō, Buddhism, Daoism and native animism. It is the philosophy and practice of true nature connection through embodiment.

Yamabushi have been practising in the Dewa Sanzan area of modern-day Yamagata for more than a thousand years. 'Dewa Sanzan' means 'the Three Mountains of Dewa' and is revered as one of the holiest places in all of Japan.

Climbing one of those mountains – Hagurosan – in silence only served to amplify the chatter in my head. I wrestled my thoughts into order in an effort to focus on why I had come. Back at the pilgrim lodge Master Hayasaka had advised, 'On the mountain we sit in meditation, but *yamabushi* meditation is not like Zen meditation. We just sit on the earth and stay there for a while. It's good to be still, but it's fine if you move. Everything in nature moves. Your eyes can be open or shut. It doesn't matter. Just be quiet and notice your experience.'

He gestured towards a small patch of ground away from the main trail, indicating where I should sit for a while. For how long, I had no idea. I simply had to be there until Master Hayasaka took up his *horagai* – a conch shell fitted with a metal mouthpiece – and blew it twice, filling the forest with the haunting call of the wild.

A shaft of sunlight fell across his *jika tabi* (white, split-toed boots), dusty from countless treks up and down this sacred peak. My own sturdy walking boots suddenly seemed chunky and rigid in comparison, as if they had been constructed to protect me from the very mountain I had come to meet. I took them off, along with my socks, and I stood for a moment on the damp cold earth. Curling golden leaves crunched beneath my pale feet. My breathing was jagged. I was six thousand miles from home, missing my family, grieving my friend, and exhausted after a relentless season of work.

Be here now. That familiar call of many ancient wisdom traditions was potent among the cedars. *But it's more complicated than that,* I heard myself saying. Ignoring my own argument, I took a seat, closed my eyes, and allowed myself to be breathed by the mountain.

Midlife malaise

According to the Office of National Statistics, my life expectancy is eighty-seven years and six months.[2] That is an average based on several factors, including the month and place I was born, but essentially, I passed the halfway mark just before my forty-fourth birthday. For the past two years, since Lisa's cancer diagnosis came thundering in just as I crossed that statistical midlife threshold, and separate from my feelings of heartbreak for Lisa's family, I had sensed a rumbling beneath the surface of my days. News like that is destabilising for anyone, and it's personal. It reminds us of our own mortality and the fragility of life.

Sometimes I tried to ignore the rumbling, especially in the light of Lisa's situation, telling myself, 'You are here. You are healthy. You don't know how lucky you are. Stop overthinking things.' But some days, news of a further decline in her health would send me the other way: 'Life is short. Are you sure you're making the most of it?'

On the days I felt brave enough to turn and face the rumbling, I saw opportunities which once lay ahead of me now discarded on the trail behind, out of reach, with no hope of retrieval, simply because I was getting older. For an optimist who has always believed deep down that the world is full of possibility, this feeling was new, and terrifying. Age was closing doors on me, one after another. I'd run towards one, and it would shut. I'd run towards another and it too would shut, taunting me as if I were trapped in some kind of hideous game.

In my twenties anything had seemed possible, I just had to decide what to do. In my thirties, with a career and travel and the arrival of children, even though it felt like there weren't enough hours in the day to do everything, I could still choose. But in my forties, it was suddenly different. I sensed that there were neither enough years left to do all the things I wanted to do, nor as many options as before because of all the decisions I had made along the way, which had cut off some things which once seemed possible. And that was assuming I did actually have half a lifetime left, an assumption that Lisa's illness had thrown into doubt.

One particular question attached itself to every thought trail:

What do I need to be doing now to ensure that when I am in my final days, whenever that may be, I will know in my heart that mine was a life well lived?

Well, that is the gentle version. It sometimes showed up as: 'How can you be more than forty years into this life, call yourself an adult, never mind a self-help author, and still have no clue what you are doing?'

Thinking about these things on repeat had only bred more questions:

- How do I know if I am doing life right?
- How can I be more efficient with my time?
- What should I do about money? Should I be making more money? Should I care less about money?
- What will I regret years from now if I don't do it at this point?
- How can I balance the pull to do meaningful work with the needs of my family?
- What if I make a choice and it is the wrong one?

And on and on . . . It was exhausting.

I was locked in a battle with myself. My ego wanted to be in control, have a plan and make it happen, be successful in the eyes of others, and build enough wealth to leave a substantial legacy when I'm gone. I had a feeling this was connected to some deep-seated beliefs about what success looks like, and what makes me feel safe in this world.

But an inner whisper told me that what I really needed to do was to let go of the desire for control, stop clinging to plans, be awake to the experience of life as it unfolds, thrive in my own eyes, and live in a way that creates a legacy in the impact I have on others each and every day. Oh, and to have more fun.

Despite how much the inner whisper resonated, my logical brain's assertions always seemed to drown it out. It was time to find a way to excavate my beliefs, deal with lingering regrets, and figure out how to navigate the rest of my life with intention. Perhaps I just needed to get away from my inbox and to-do list, and the constant barrage of news, social media noise and other people's opinions long enough to really listen for some answers.

Japan calling

One wet afternoon, I was folding paper chatterboxes with my children, half-distracted by these musings, when I had the strangest sensation of leaving my own body and looking back on the three of us from the corner of our kitchen. I saw myself hunched at the counter, there but not really there, folding squares of white paper while the girls chatted, their brightness highlighting the greyness of my own being.

A cloud shifted, changing the shadows on the table. The square origami sheet in my hands became a visual representation of my expected lifespan of nearly eighty-eight years. I saw myself folding it in half lengthways into two rectangles of forty-four years each, and then folding it in half again. Each square, small enough to fit in my pocket, contained a quarter lifetime of twenty-two years.

Twenty-two. My quarter-life threshold. Back then, I had been living and working in Yamagata, a remote snowy part of northern Japan I had been drawn to because of its name, which means 'mountain form'. I drifted into the memory, and then back to the kitchen. I saw myself unfolding the paper and refolding it, and then my imagination took over again and the white square was reworking itself like an animated puzzle, taking the shape of three paper peaks.

Dewa Sanzan. Of course. The area known as the Three Mountains of Dewa, in the heart of Yamagata, has been a place of domestic pilgrimage and spiritual training for more than a thousand years. Hagurosan, 'Black Wing Mountain', is known as the mountain of the present and earthly desires. Gassan, 'Moon Mountain', represents death and the past. And Yudonosan, 'Sacred Spring Mountain', is the mountain of rebirth and the future.

Suddenly, I knew I had to go back.

As the universe would have it, Japan's national borders, which had been shut for more than two years due to the Covid-19 pandemic, were just about to reopen. I said my goodbyes and took the next plane east.

I accept (anything and everything)

As I sat rooted to the mountain in meditation, my breath gently washed away the noise in my head, and time folded in on itself. When at last I heard the call of the *horagai*, it seemed to come from the depths of the ocean and everywhere in the forest all at once.

In keeping with *yamabushi* protocol, the only way I was permitted to respond to the call of the conch was to say '*uketamō*', which means 'I accept (anything and everything)'. Whatever presented itself on this mountain, I must accept it. The weather. My body's response to the climb. The emotions that arose and dissipated with each moment like fish bubbles in a river.

Sendatsu, the respectful name for my senior *yamabushi* guide, set quite a pace once we were back on the path. I followed, making awkward music with my wooden staff on the stone staircase that had been set into the mountainside some four centuries ago. With each footstep, laid over the ghostly imprints of millions of pilgrims before me, I sensed a tethering of my earthly body to an entire community of ancestors in one direction, and to the mountain in the other. This was not a common feeling for me,

focused as I tend to be in the currency of the modern world, and
yet it held the comforting echo of some primal familiarity, an
umbilical cord nourishing me from a source far away.

I had read that *yamabushi* have an important role as connec-
tors, braiding people to the land, to spirits, to nature and to
each other, weaving a sense of sacredness and remembrance into
daily life. Every now and then, Master Hayasaka would blow on
the *horagai*, sending long draughts of sound into the sky, like a
memory of the river which once carried minerals from this very
mountain to the sea, and in time formed conch shells like the
one he uses now, to turn his own breath into resonant wind.
Elements transformed.

Earth, water, fire, wind, void. The five elements that make up
the universe, according to esoteric Japanese Buddhism. On the
way up the mountain we had paid our respects at the Gojyū-no-
tō, the famous five-storeyed pagoda which stands among ancient
cedars at the base of Hagurosan. On one of my previous visits, an
official had told me how the five storeys of the pagoda symbolise
earth (*chi*) at the bottom, rising through water (*sui*), fire (*ka*), wind
(*fū*) and void (*kū*), closest to the sky.

I recalled how I had asked a Japanese friend for his definition
of *kū*. Suzuki-san lifted his arm and swooshed it in a wide arc.
'You know how in Noh theatre an actor moves his sleeve in a slow
dramatic sweep, and that in doing so, he creates an opening for
the story to unfold? That is *kū*.' And I smiled, and remembered
why I love the Japanese language.

He continued, 'It's the same with *sumi-e* painting. We only
use black ink, and if you add too much and fill the page, there
can only be one story. The thing becomes fixed. But if you allow
enough white space, there is room for the viewer's own interpretation to flower in their imagination, and the painting can

generate many stories. In esoteric Buddhism, the element of *kū* is essential. The existence of the potentiality allows a widening of perspective.'

Perhaps that was what was missing from my life at the moment: I had been so busy building things, and doing things, and worrying about the things I could no longer do, that I had not left any white space for what might be, for all that was still unknown.

Now, as I trod the stone path, winding through the forest, inhaling the mountain air, a feeling of spaciousness opened up somewhere in my chest.

Unfinished business

Several years ago I wrote a book called *Wabi Sabi: Japanese wisdom for a perfectly imperfect life*. In it, I explored the beauty of imperfection and what the concept of *wabi sabi* could teach us about acceptance and letting go. What I have never told anyone is that on submitting the manuscript, I was left with a sense of something being incomplete, but I was not sure what.

Towards the end of *Wabi Sabi* I had shared an experience of time slowing to the point I could almost see a new memory being imprinted on my heart. I wrote about it to illustrate a point, without realising that reliving it had loosened the ribbon on an old scroll of questions I had gathered in my twenties and thirties, but had rolled up and put away when I got busy with my career and, later, with family life. Questions about time and meaning, mortality and mystery, and how to navigate life so we have no regrets.

As I hit send on the *Wabi Sabi* manuscript, got up from my chair and turned to the window of my attic writing room, the forgotten scroll fell from my lap and unravelled, spilling the questions all over the floor. I knelt and gathered them up carefully, knowing that as one story finished, another was just beginning.

'What do you think happens when you die?' Lisa had asked me. I told her I didn't know. Nobody knows. 'I guess I'll find out in about six weeks,' she said, with a hollow laugh. 'If no miracle comes, I'll know. If a miracle comes, I'm going to live fully. Either way, it will be the end of this particular time.'

Her clarity was astonishing. *Either way, it will be the end of this particular time.* It made me think of all the occasions I had moved from one phase of life to another without realising I was crossing a threshold, where a 'last time' now belonged in the 'before'. The last time I saw my grandma alive. The last time I breastfed my youngest child. The last day I was young, before I became middle-aged.

> **Even though we have a sense of what we mean by 'midlife', and we might have a sense of our life expectancy, the truth is we never know how long we have left, so we never know when we are halfway through.**

On Mount Haguro, remembering Lisa's words, I was overcome with a feeling that I was facing a choice: midlife would not last for ever, and I could either see it as a fog to stumble through, ignoring the gnawing questions and exhausting myself through striving for success in the eyes of the world (or at least to avoid becoming irrelevant in the eyes of the world), or I could see it as a doorway to step through intentionally, not knowing what lay beyond, but quietly trusting that a picture of true success would reveal itself – perhaps in the shape of a life well lived.

A distant call

On the way back down we paused beside a tree so old and beloved it has been given a name: Jijisugi, the Grandpa Cedar. A twisted length of rope known as a *shimenawa* was tied around its mighty thousand-year-old trunk to indicate its sacred status. I got shivers as I thought of how, back in the seventeenth century, one of my favourite haiku poets, Matsuo Bashō, passed this very same tree on his own long, hard passage through these mountains, pausing nearby to pen a poem about a moment so still, he could smell the snow.[3]

It is said that Bashō's experience at Dewa Sanzan led him to the epiphany of *fueki-ryūkō*, the principle of balancing immutability and fluidity that would characterise haiku from that day on.[4] This tension of the constant and the changing is one I grapple with daily. I feel the paradox of continuity as a human being (that I have been me in this body since I was born) and the knowledge that I am not the same person from day to day, moment to moment. I am certainly not the same person I was when I first climbed Hagurosan, half a lifetime ago.

My sense of the mountain had barely changed. Still mysterious and dark, timeless and inviting, air always heavy with the scent of moss and prayers. But in recent years the world beyond the mountain has changed in so many ways. We seem to have become at once more technologically connected and more socially separated. Everything has sped up. Some of this feeling is likely a product of my life stage; days are often a piecing together of multiple schedules, in constant pursuit of something other than what is right here. We seem to have become slaves to time, tangled up in it, governed by it, at its mercy yet always wanting more. In our world of life hacks and time-management solutions, something is missing.

The head-driven tendencies of my own culture lend themselves to alignment with linear time, but at Dewa Sanzan, I sensed that I might be missing something with my allegiance to this approach.

I felt like I had been climbing away from the first half of my life, which had been – as it is for so many of us – characterised by cravings and desire, which emanate from the thinking mind. Passing through the statistical mid-point had been like crashing through a rice-paper wall, the boundary pierced and unrepairable, the tearing revealing a whole new space on the other side. And now I felt pulled towards something else, something I could not yet articulate. A longing which came from some other place. From the *kokoro*, perhaps.

The *yatagarasu* was back, cawing from somewhere deep in the forest. It was my turn to follow.

KOKORO WORK: LIFE

- Where are you in your life right now? In what ways is this different or similar to how you imagined your life would be at this particular age and stage?
- What tensions or conflicting priorities are real for you right now? (Don't judge, just write them down.)
- What questions about life won't leave you alone? (You don't have to answer them, just write the questions down.)

KOKORO WISDOM

A life well lived is a life well examined.

Reflect on your life regularly, and check in
with how you feel about each aspect of it. If
something feels off, investigate that feeling, which
is an important message from your *kokoro*.

CHAPTER 2

HEART-MINDFULNESS

Just arranging flowers

On Mount Haguro that day, I had been searching for symbols carved into the stone steps. The simple line drawings of gourds, lotus flowers, sake cups and bottles have been there for centuries, and many have been worn to vanishing under the footprints of pilgrims. It is said that if you find all thirty-three your wishes will come true. At one point, I was staring so hard at the mossy wet steps ahead of me that my climb became almost trance-like, and I saw the character for *kokoro* appear. At least I thought I did, until I realised it was just a group of fractures in the stone.

Do you ever have that? When a word, phrase, symbol or idea arises unbidden over and over until you pay attention? For some time, whenever I had tried to approach my midlife malaise with anything other than direct thinking – doing yoga, writing, meditating, taking a question for a walk and so on – the same thing happened. One particular word would appear at the edges of my consciousness, either as four inked strokes of a Chinese character, 心, or as the sound of three syllables: *Kokoro*.

The evidence was there in the margins of my notebooks. It was like a beloved dog, padding alongside me as I walked up the river, noticing the seasons change. It was a refrain so constant that I started to take notice. What did *kokoro* have to teach me, and why now?

*

The word *kokoro* has been alive in the Japanese language since before there was a system to write it down. It is one of the original words in the ancient tongue known as *yamato kotoba*, which was spoken in Japan during the Yamato period (250–710 CE) when the Imperial court ruled from the modern-day Nara Prefecture.

Chinese characters, known in Japanese as *kanji*, travelled across the sea from China on swords, seals, coins and correspondence, taking hold as the official writing system of Japan somewhere around the late fifth or early sixth century.[1] The word *kokoro* came to be written 心, and given the alternative reading of *shin* (from the Chinese *xīn*).

The simplest translation of *kokoro* is 'heart'. However, distinct from the physical organ of the heart – which is *shinzō* (心臓) in Japanese – *kokoro* represents the spiritual aspect of a human being. Alternative translations often found in martial arts and cultural settings include 'mind', 'spirit' and 'heart-mind'. In fact, *kokoro* is all of these things.

Some describe it as the thinking aspect of the heart, others as the feeling aspect of the mind, or the embodied spirit. There are those who say it is the seat of the soul. The origin of our inner knowing. The storehouse of our emotions.

The *kokoro* is the intelligent heart, which communicates our innate wisdom and responds to the world in the form of felt impulses.

The *kokoro* is the internal place from which a human responds sensitively to the world through the language of felt energetic impulses rather than rational thought, and where we are engaged in the present instead of being pulled into the past or future by the regrets or worries of the monkey mind, or pulled onto a different path by the expectations and opinions of others.

The *kokoro* is a mechanism for accessing the soul's intelligence and our deepest wisdom. It is the source of our innate capacity for feeling the innermost nature of things (which join us to each other and the world we live in), as well as the source of our natural creative response to the world. In Japanese culture, the understanding of this felt language of the *kokoro* is absolutely essential in navigating relationships, appreciating beauty and responding to the world from moment to moment.

The term can be used as 'the *kokoro*' in the sense of its being an entity – one which is both generative and responsive. When you witness beauty or sorrow, for example, and sense a flutter or a tightening, that is an utterance of your *kokoro*. It can also be used in the sense of something measurable; for example, 'to have a wealth of *kokoro*' means to have a spiritually rich life as opposed to a materially rich life.

Japan's most popular dictionary, *Kōjien*, begins a long list of definitions of *kokoro* with the description 'the origin of a human's spiritual actions, or those actions themselves'.[2] In the *Concise Oxford Dictionary of World Religions*, *kokoro* is explained as 'the fundamental and interior nature of a person, thus virtually equivalent to Buddha-nature'.[3] It can also mean the centre, nucleus or core of something. It is how we see, respond to and create beauty.

It was this single character, *kokoro*, hand-brushed like the shortest of poems and framed in black, which greeted me at the entrance to Igo-sensei's dojo (school of traditional and martial arts), in north Kyoto one bright autumnal day.

Kokoro as compass

'I study as if I'm going to live to 120, and I live as if today is all I have.' Before I even had the chance to open my notebook, Igo-sensei had summarised her approach to life in a single sentence. At seventy-eight, the same age as my mother, Igo-sensei was an Aikido Master, an ikebana (flower-arranging) teacher, and an accomplished tea connoisseur. She has been teaching children about Japanese culture for almost half a century, and is still active today. We met at the dojo she claimed she never planned to own, but rather took on when the opportunity arose. She just knew it was the next right thing to do. It turned out this has been something of a pattern in her life.

Igo-sensei was calm and assured, funny and self-deprecating as she related her extraordinary life path. It was a story of immense challenges – illness, career changes, and a heavy burden of caring for others – but it was also the winding path of someone who has embraced life at every turn whatever has been thrown her way.

As she was talking, Igo-sensei seemed to have the realisation that she has never been a planner, never set a goal and gone after it, but instead has felt her way through the world. Whenever she has been drawn to something, she has followed that sense towards it. Hers was not the story of a dreamer or a strategist, but of someone completely alive to each unfolding situation, acutely attuned to her *kokoro*'s response to the moment and the new possibilities it presented.

Her dojo offers lessons not only in aikido but in the tea ceremony and flower arranging too. If that weren't enough, Igo-sensei, who has Parkinson's, has just taken up the piano both for the joy of music and to help manage her symptoms. She said, 'It's best to do what you want to, while you still can.'

This reminds me of something Lisa said just a few weeks before she died. We were chatting on Zoom, me in my office, her at the hospice. I asked her what she had been up to that day. 'Sitting in the sun, writing some notes, doing a bit of my aromatherapy course,' she said. 'I know what you're thinking,' she continued. 'What's the point?' I said nothing but squirmed in shame. The thought had apparently crossed my face. She explained, 'I'm not doing it out of some kind of false hope or because it might be useful in the future. I'm doing it because it's interesting now.'

During the last year of her life, Lisa realised something simple but important: joy alone is reason enough to do anything. She said, 'I love collecting things and for a long time I thought it was weird to get so much joy from it, so I judged myself while doing it. But recently I have come to realise that it is actually the simple things that bring me the most joy. Watching the stars, being in nature, walking, collecting things, craft. I don't have to discover a new star, or walk the furthest, or win a crafting prize. For someone like me, who likes a little bit of everything, it has been a revelation to realise that it's okay just to do something because you enjoy it, and not always have to achieve something as a result.'

Joy is one of the many feelings that blooms in the *kokoro*. When we make decisions guided by this sense of what blooms in us, we navigate life in a different way. Our days look different, and we feel different at the end of each one. We might call this feeling approach 'heart-mindfulness'. We don't make a conscious decision to feel a certain way, the feeling just arises, and we are aware of its arising.

To be heart-mindful is to tune in to the moment, focusing on what we feel in a particular situation, and responding from there. It is where direct observation and logical thinking give way to a felt sense of the world, and the narrative falls away.

When we approach life heart-mindfully,
we experience the joy of arranging
flowers, while understanding we are
never really just arranging flowers.

To approach your day heart-mindfully is to walk with sensitivity to, and awareness of, the aliveness in everything around you, in the knowledge that nothing lasts for ever, and all will eventually fade. It is also to recognise the feelings that arise in you in response to the world, as you encounter it in each and every moment.

Writing has been one of my greatest teachers in this regard. In time, practising heart-mindfulness gets easier, and we can begin to trust the intelligence that arises from within.

Kokoro as voice

The Kawamura Noh Theatre[4] was unrecognisable from my last visit. Dozens of stunning kimono were strung up between wooden posts where the audience usually sat, like washing lines hung with costumes worth as much as small cars. Hand-stitched butterflies on crimson silk, golden swirls like ripples on a lake of pale blue, tiny flowers and flowing grasses in pinks, purples and greens on a swathe of indigo.

The gallery was filled with rows of ribbons, lines of long black wigs, and a huge collection of obi belts cascading over the banister. The stage was covered, on the left with more than fifty fans edged in gold, each resting on its case, and on the right with more than 120 Noh masks, fashioned from wood and finished using a powder made from the crushed shells of sea creatures.

Noh masks are believed to have spirits of their own, so they must be treated with the utmost reverence. Laid out as they were in lines, each placed carefully on the fabric bag it was usually stored in, I couldn't help thinking that they looked like people buried up to their necks in sand, each having a different experience. Some looked relaxed, others exhausted. Some had an inquisitive countenance, others seemed aloof. Some appeared terrified, others – especially those with horns – were terrifying to me. Some looked like the faces of young people, others were older. I had never seen anything like it.

Kneeling on the floor in a black kimono was Master of Noh, Haruhisa Kawamura, holding up a mask that had been used for more than six hundred years. This lively actor had generously opened up his theatre for a handful of us to observe the annual *mushi boshi* – the airing of every element of the elaborate Noh costumes, to dry them out, remove any insects and preserve the items for years to come. It was a rare opportunity to go behind the scenes of one of the world's oldest performing arts, a tradition that has been alive for more than half a millennium.

Picking out a mask with fluid curves that was used when playing the part of a middle-aged woman, Master Kawamura explained how such a mask, seemingly of fixed expression, can actually communicate many shades of the human condition – subject to the actor's skill, of course.

'In most cultures masks are used to hide the emotional truth of the person behind them,' he said, 'but in Noh it is the opposite. The mask, called the *omote* [meaning "surface"], draws out the actor's emotions and actually facilitates their projection out to the audience.'

The art of Noh comes from the *kokoro* of the actor, and seeks to have an effect on the *kokoro* of audience members. Noh actor and playwright Zeami Motokiyo (1363–1443) spoke of 'opening the *kokoro* ear' of the audience through the power and feeling of the *kokoro* of the actors.[5] According to Noh research by Japanese art and religion specialist Professor Richard B. Pilgrim, 'The various layers and kinds of *kokoro* are unified in a spiritual/mental/ emotional wholeness which arises out of and expresses the very depths of being. Neither art nor man is a stratification of separate parts, but a diversity which ultimately expresses a unity founded on the very essence of life.'[6]

Kokoro as mirror

A few days later, I was sheltering from the rain at The Good Day Velo Bikes & Coffee,[7] on a back street in central Kyoto. Naoki-san, the owner, was taking his time preparing a pour-over coffee. We are a similar age, and the first time I walked into his tiny two-bench cafe I stayed for hours. Father to a young son and a cancer survivor, Naoki-san set up his business in order to have a slower life, where he always has time for people.

That day, there was no rush. I was the only customer. The rain showed no signs of easing, and our conversation drifted from the best hidden places for *momiji*[8] viewing to the naming of our children, from stories of our ancestors to my ongoing enquiry about the *kokoro*.

'I like your music,' I said. 'It's very relaxing. I should go really. I have many things to do but ... I'm just going to sit here until the rain stops.'

'That's my concept,' Naoki-san said, laughing.

'Before I go, can I ask, when you hear the word *kokoro* what do you think of?'

I had no idea what Naoki-san was going to say, and I certainly wasn't expecting this.

'The *kokoro* is a kind of mirror,' he said. 'It's what other people see when they look at you. If your heart is dirty, people know. They can sense it. I try to be respectful to everyone. It doesn't matter who they are. I try to keep my *kokoro* clean. And if I get frustrated by something or someone, I often go to a temple or a shrine to reset my *kokoro*, to purify it. I don't pray or anything, I just go there, spend some time surrounded by nature and it somehow reminds me that I am part of something bigger. Then I go back to our house.

'Like today,' he continued. 'Today my business is slow and I'm frustrated. I can't go home in this state of *kokoro*, so on my way back I will go to the Kamogawa River and reset. I will clean my *kokoro*, and then I can go home with a smile. I can hug my son, I can say thank you to my wife. I can say thank you for my life.

'That's what I think of when I think of *kokoro*. Just trying to be a good father, a good person, a good shop owner.'

Curious, I probed a little. 'If you don't do that, what happens?'

'If I don't do it and then I go home, I am still angry. I don't talk to my son or my wife. I just think about my business. I am focused on tomorrow, worried about what I should do next. I don't want to be like that, so I try to actively purify my *kokoro* whenever I need to. I just go somewhere peaceful – it doesn't have to be a temple or shrine. I might go to the river or to the mountains. Anywhere in nature is good. I go there and say thank you for the day.'

'That's beautiful,' I said, meaning it.

He smiled and passed me another coffee. 'It's a very Japanese thing to do.'

Kokoro as window

A few days later, I was invited to give a presentation to a group
of Kyoto residents who are active in the protection of the city's
heritage. Most of the group were in their eighties, and the chair
was ninety-two. All of them had enjoyed distinguished careers
in engineering, government, architecture and science, and I was
expecting a technical analysis of the *kokoro* in response to the
questions I posed to the group at the end. In fact what ensued
was a surprisingly soulful discussion.

When I mentioned Naoki-san's image of the *kokoro* as a mirror,
one of the group revealed his belief that the *kokoro* is the vehicle
for the soul's projection outwards. 'I think of it like a window,' he
said. 'If the window is clouded with heavy, negative emotions, the
soul's light cannot be projected into the world.' And in reverse,
we cannot clearly access the soul's intelligence.

I loved this idea of the *kokoro* as a window. In one direction,
we can peer into our inner life, and in the other, we can express
the wisdom and beauty of that inner life out in the world.

Joining in the conversation, his friend Yokoyama-san said
he sees it in yet another way. Every morning, come rain, shine,
heatwave or snow, Yokoyama-san leaves his house in the dark
and heads to Demachiyanagi, where the river divides, to watch
the sun rise over the Higashiyama mountains. He has done this
for decades, and says that he feels like he receives the light of the
world into his *kokoro* each morning, enabling him to beam light
back out to others throughout the day.

The following week, I dropped round to Yokoyama-san's
house for tea and he told me he had been chatting to a monk
from Bukkōji Temple about my questions. He said he'd shared
his idea of the *kokoro* as a kind of machine that transmutes the

energy of light, and the monk had just nodded and said, 'Sounds about right.'

> It is the *kokoro* that makes us human,
> and it is the light of the *kokoro* which
> guides us along an authentic life path.

It was becoming clear to me that the *kokoro* is a dynamic and vital part of us as human beings, and as such we need to take good care of it; something I had been neglecting to do.

As my midlife malaise had built over the past couple of years, I had sensed a shortening of my temper and a lowering of my tolerance for noise in general and for bickering in particular. Sometimes I caught myself talking harshly to people I loved and wondered who was saying those things in such a way, even as the words were falling from my mouth. Perhaps my *kokoro* was cloudy. I certainly hadn't been soaking up the light of the universe or beaming it out to others much lately.

Listening to Naoki-san and the group of wise elders, I realised I needed to find a way to bring this light bathing and *kokoro* cleansing into my daily routine, not just for myself but for my family, too. It was time to seek out stillness somewhere peaceful, and see what wisdom might arise in the silence. Fortunately, Japan is one of the best places in the world for such a pursuit, and I knew exactly where to go.

KOKORO WORK: HEART-MINDFULNESS

- In which areas of your life do you tend to overthink things? What might be different if you allowed yourself to tune in to the wisdom of your *kokoro*? Try practising heart-mindfulness, then write down any reflections.
- Think of a recent situation where you have carried negative emotions from one space to another. How could you have cleansed your *kokoro* in between to avoid contaminating the new situation? How might this have been good both for you and others affected?
- Who do you know who lives guided by their *kokoro*? In what ways do they inspire you? What could you learn from them?

KOKORO WISDOM

A life well lived is a life experienced heart-mindfully.

Instead of going through life analysing and judging everything with our rational minds, experiencing life heart-mindfully – from the *kokoro* – tunes us in to the beauty, joy and wonder right in front of us and helps us navigate from moment to moment according to how we feel.

CHAPTER 3

STILLNESS

Where silence speaks

'Life, less than a hundred years, floats like a boat on a river,'[1] mused the bow-tie-wearing taxi driver striding ahead of me, repeating one of my favourite lines of poetry. It was a strange response to my question as to whether he was sure he could spare the time to accompany me to my destination on foot, but I think he meant that life is short and unpredictable, and serendipitous encounters are to be enjoyed. Mr Tsuji was quoting Zen monk and poet Ryōkan Taigu (1758–1831), whose hermitage we were on our way to visit.

I had only met Mr Tsuji half an hour earlier, when I had hopped into his taxi outside Tsubame-Sanjō station in rural Niigata. As we drove through miles of rice fields he remarked how curious it was that I wanted to go to Gogōan[2], the hut where Ryōkan settled at the age of forty, shortly after his father's death. 'It's one of my favourite places,' he said, 'but no one ever asks to be taken there. And here you are, a foreigner, having come all this way to see it.' I explained how I loved Ryōkan's poetry, how it often led me to a place of stillness in my mind in a way I could not quite explain. I was interested to see where such a poet might have lived.

We had parked near the base of Mount Kugami. Mr Tsuji had turned off the meter and declared that as he had nothing to do for the rest of the afternoon, he would be glad to guide me up the mountain. As we climbed – me in waterproof trousers and muddy walking boots, him in shiny black shoes and a crease-less blue suit – he told me what he knew of Ryōkan's life, and how the poet had spent much of his time living alone in a small hermitage in the grounds of Kokujōji Temple here on Mount Kugami, from time to time taking the long walk to the village for *takuhatsu* (begging). His lifestyle was only possible because of the generosity of the villagers, yet accounts of the time note how Ryōkan's *takuhatsu* was also an opportunity for those villagers to let go of their attachment to their relative wealth, as they gave him whatever they could spare.[3] For Ryōkan, on the receiving end, it was a practice of constant acceptance. He had no choice about what arrived in his bowl.

Besides being renowned as a poet and calligrapher, Ryōkan had a reputation for fun. He would often put down his begging bowl to play with local children, who were the source of much joy for him, a scene immortalised in the form of a playful statue high on the mountain.

Rejecting any societal expectation, Ryōkan lived a simple life. He befriended the moon and the maples, read poetry, listened to the rain and wrote about it. The words he left behind indicate a gentle awareness of the contrasts which coloured life in his flimsy hut – joy and loneliness, shadow and light, lack and abundance. His poetry is uncomplicated yet beautiful, and it gets to the heart of things.

The path was a series of thick stones set into the mountain, steep and overgrown in places, with sprawling networks of tree roots on show. Ryōkan alternately lamented and celebrated being cut off from news of the affairs of men[4] and having nothing of substance to report about his own life. Yet some of his poems contain sage life advice, encouraging us to stop chasing worldly things if we want to find true meaning. As I climbed I realised that besides a curiosity about how Ryōkan lived and a deep yearning for the stillness I sensed in his poems, it was this desire to stop chasing that had brought me to Mount Kugami.

Mr Tsuji and I paused to rest on a fallen tree trunk and take in lungfuls of forest air. I took out a box of Pocky from my rucksack and shared the chocolate-dipped pretzel sticks, feeling like a small child on a secret adventure with a new friend.

When at last we arrived at the hermitage, we found a simple wooden structure raised off the ground, open on two sides and surrounded by trees. Rebuilt since Ryōkan's time, the hut had settled into its surroundings and the thatched roof was covered in moss. These days there is no furniture except for a small *butsudan* altar, but if you had dropped in for tea at the rebel poet's hut at the turn of the nineteenth century, you might have noticed a small desk to the side, carrying a lamp, a single ink stone and brush, and a small stack of beloved books, including the writings of Zen Master Eihei Dōgen, who he greatly admired. You might have heard a wild animal crying deep in the mountains[5], or found comfort in the sound of snowfall, just as Ryōkan did.

I stepped up into the hut and sat down on the smooth floorboards, looking out at the view that had inspired so many poems. Mr Tsuji took himself off to lean against a tree, leaving me alone in the hut. I could hear birds calling and leaves rustling. A physical silence entered my body.

According to writer Kōji Nakano, Ryōkan wasn't good at the minutiae of life: 'He would direct a penetrating gaze into the deep recesses of his heart, looking always and only at absolute problems, those transcending time and place ... The heart is the target of Buddhism and, as Dōgen saw it, the place where the Buddha resides. This became Ryōkan's view as well.'[6]

Day-to-day worries and to-do lists and other ruminations (*Do this. Reply to this. Analyse what so-and-so meant by this . . .*) vie for our attention with the external noise of the modern world (*Watch this. 'Like' this. Buy this . . .*). Much of this is generated by or captured on the smartphones we willingly keep close by at all times. We spend our attention to validate our experiences, boost our self-esteem and prove our worth.

Sitting on the floor of Ryōkan's hut, on a mountainside far from home, with no mobile reception or internet access, I understood how this noise is a constant pull to be visible. These days, visibility is so often equated to value – status, presenteeism, possessions on show, achievements shouted out loud, follower numbers, constant reporting of what we have been doing and so on, not to mention the degree to which we respond to those who demand our attention.

As a small business owner, I constantly feel this pressure – to post regularly on social media, to send newsletters, to brag about success in order to sell things. I understand the importance of this for building trust with people who don't know me, and I am aware that if I don't tell people about the things I have poured my heart into creating, those things cannot help or inspire them; but the constant launching, promoting and pushing for-wards is exhausting, and the value placed on visibility makes me uncomfortable.

There on the mountain, I sensed that perhaps there are some things that have been unknowingly cast aside in the wake of my own striving, which might have value to me personally – if only I could pause long enough to turn around and gather them up. Things like private moments of beauty, connection, peace and wonder.

There is nothing to do on the mountain
other than the work of the *kokoro*. To rest
in stillness and be there, experiencing
your place in the great web of things.

Having seen where Ryōkan lived, I now understood that his
genius was in truly noticing the moment in front of him, and
in being aware of how his heart responded to it. He paid attention and wrote it down. Ryōkan's poetry is lyrical and deep, yet
straightforward. In just a few lines he manages to capture both
the beauty of the natural world and the transient nature of life.
I thought about how we often strive so hard with our creativity,
battling fear as we push for perfection, while doubting deeply
both the quality of what we produce and our own self-worth. I
wondered how much easier it might be if we just spilt what is in
our hearts, without editing or judging before it hit the page, or
splashed onto the canvas. Perhaps a path of ease might open up if
we simply surrendered to the moment, let go of all striving, and
just put on paper – in words or images – what we see, feel and
experience of the world as it arises. Perhaps the beauty is already
there, outside and within us, simply waiting to be laid down.

Inside Ryōkan's hut, I felt far away from work obligations,
deadlines, any kind of manmade urgency or the call to visibility.
As strange as it sounds, I actually felt somehow wiser there; as if
listening to nature with the entirety of my being on the land that
had inspired one of Japan's most famous poets had unlocked some
wisdom I did not realise I had been carrying. Or perhaps I had just
heard the echo of Ryōkan's ghost, whispering poetry on the wind.

SIMPLE WAYS TO TUNE IN TO YOUR *KOKORO*

- Slow down and pay attention to what is right in front of you.
- Be curious – notice what interests you, even if it seems to have no bankable value, and explore that.
- Find space and stillness and actively listen with your whole body.
- Meditate.
- Keep a journal and notice the themes you keep returning to.
- Pay more attention to your inner life.
- Explore creative activities that allow your *kokoro* to communicate your inner wisdom through expression.
- Be aware of where you are being influenced by external views that do not feel in alignment with what matters to you.
- Practise listening from your body when you have to make a decision. Ask yourself a question and try on different answers to see if they 'feel' right.

Finding space

Having bid farewell to Mr Tsuji, I caught a train onwards. As it rumbled through the countryside, rice fields tumbled by, and I had a memory of a feeling.

Several years earlier, when my youngest child was so small it was a desperate wrench to be away from her, I had joined a nature quest[7] in England's Lake District at the invitation of a friend who knew better than me how much I needed it. I had travelled there by train, and on the return journey I had a particular feeling in my chest that I felt again on that train travelling away from Ryōkan's hut.

For the nature quest, I had to spend thirty hours alone on a hillside, inside a circle some twenty metres or so in diameter. I was not allowed my phone, any food or company, not even a notebook to write in. I measured out the circle with my strides and, as I had been instructed, did a ceremony to each of the four directions. Then I sat, staring over the hills, wondering what to do with the remaining twenty-nine hours.

Over the hill came a flock of angry sheep who didn't want me on their land, but I couldn't move my circle now that the clock was ticking. I had made a commitment. The largest of the sheep started to bleat loudly and the others joined in. I urgently searched the archives of my mind for stories of middle-aged women attacked by sheep on a remote hillside and was relieved not to find any. Instead, I found the words for Christmas carols, and I started to sing. First 'Silent Night', then 'Away in a Manger' and 'Little Donkey'. By the time I got to 'Once in Royal David's City', the sheep had stopped bleating and started to eat the grass, perfectly lined up as they were around the edges of my unmarked circle.

I settled into my space on the hillside and breathed deeply, animal companions at my side. The gap was a boundaried opening in the flow of my days, which were very full with parenting two small children, building a business and earning enough to pay for city life. The nature quest was an opportunity to take a breath before diving back in. Life was held back at the edges of the pause, just as the invisible circle had somehow held back the sheep, honouring the space I needed. In the Japanese language this 'space' is called *ma* and written 間 with a character that combines the foundational *kanji* component (門), known as the gate radical, with the character for sun (日).

The space represented by the word *ma* is an important concept in art and architecture, music, martial arts, ikebana, Zen garden design, in the tea ceremony and in conversation. *Ma* is a gap in a rushed life, the pause between stimulus and calm response. It is the space between us.

The character for *ma* can also be read *aida*. Playwright Chikamatsu Monzaemon famously said, 'The truth is found in the space in between.'[8] Mirroring this, the *sumi* ink artist Tōkō Shinoda, who lived to a few days shy of 108, once wrote, '*Shinjitsu wa kanjiru kokoro ni aru*', which means 'The truth is found in the feeling *kokoro*.'[9] Perhaps the *kokoro* is found in that space in between what is explicitly said and definitely known – in the stillness, in the silence, in the gap. Or perhaps the space is defined by the *kokoro* itself.

Ma is the space that is generated by the boundaries around it. Contemporary architect Arata Isozaki has referred to this as 'the pregnant nothing.'[10] When we can find this spaciousness in our own lives, it can act as a fertile void, from which newness can arise.

Curiously, the character for *ma*, which is usually read *kan* when in combination with other characters, combines with *kū* (空), meaning 'void' or 'emptiness', to make *kūkan* (空間), meaning 'space'. In combination with *ji* (時), the counter for hours, it becomes *jikan* (時間), which means 'time'. Space and time, overlapping, just like they do in the present moment, where spaciousness can be felt.

Spaciousness located in the *kokoro* can be a doorway through which the light shines in, or a window through which our light can shine out.

I had forgotten about my hillside experience until it bubbled back up on that train in Niigata, when I noticed a feeling of spaciousness in my chest once again. How had I forgotten about the sheep and the circle and the shift? Because this is what happens in a busy life. We have a precious experience that teaches us something; we feel inspired and perhaps even vow to put our new learning into practice every day. We do it for a while, and then life speeds up again and we forget. And so the lesson returns. Of all the lessons that have returned to me in midlife, the most regular visitor is this reminder of my deep-seated need for space and stillness. I don't want to forget about it any longer.

I lived alone throughout my twenties and my early thirties, and spent a lot of time travelling, also alone. I slept in deserts, sailed oceans, stayed up late, did whatever I wanted when I wanted. But family life and building a business changed all that. The exception has been when I have taken time away from it all to write books. Perhaps part of the reason I write books is to have a good excuse to be alone in beautiful places, pondering big questions about life without interruption. I know now, deep in my bones, that this spaciousness matters not just as a way to get books written, but as an essential part of life – a counter to the noise, the pause that makes the music.

In her book *Kokoro Ni Naru Oto* ('The Sound that Rings in my Heart'), classical pianist Kikuko Kurose made a fascinating observation about how creating a rest between notes in music takes even more energy than it takes to create the notes themselves. She wrote: 'I am interested in how to give meaning to the rests', and something about those words lingered long after I had finished reading them.[11]

Zen retreat

Waiting for the ferry to Iwaya Port a few days later, the sun was shining, light was bouncing off the water and I could feel all sorts of memories bubbling up. I grew up in a port town and there's something about seeing the sea that makes me feel calm somewhere deep inside.

Iwaya was quite run-down. The shop across from the boarding gate had windows so dirty I couldn't tell what it sold. The pull-down canopy was all torn, and rubbish blew about in the doorway. The whole building needed a paint job, but somehow it looked at ease, comfortable in its shabbiness.

Waiting at the dock, I felt more relaxed than I had in a long time. Perhaps it was the slow pace of the town, or the warm sun on my skin. Or perhaps it was the prospect of spending time at a wellbeing retreat in a purpose-built meditation space on the lush island of Awaji, which was where I was heading.

Designed by architect Shigeru Ban, Zenbō Seinei[12] (lit. 'tranquil monk's dwelling') is an accommodation space specifically intended for meditation, yoga and quiet contemplation. The narrow wooden building has a 100-metre-long floating meditation deck with 360-degree panoramic views of the forest. There is a clear glass balustrade all the way around, but no walls, so the entire space is open to the elements. The deck sits atop rooms and a restaurant serving exquisite *shōjin ryōri* (vegetarian Buddhist food). At the base of the building is a shallow open-air pool filled with hot spring water.

I was greeted with a welcome drink of green tea, along with pickled plums and a small plate of nuts and goji berries. I enjoyed it sitting in a chair with a smooth, curved back that offered perfect support. Any remaining tension fell away from my shoulders and

I sat there feeling grateful for everyone who had helped to make it possible for me to be there, in that moment, in the sun.

After a while, someone came to show me to my room. As I followed him down the long corridor, inhaling the scent of *hinoki* wood, I noticed that all the rooms had beautiful names, many of them taken from Zen sayings, calligraphed on wooden signs by each sliding door. Reading each one in turn felt like a series of important reminders: *Kōin Yanogotoshi* (光陰矢如): 'time flies'; *Shogyō Mujyō* (諸行無常): 'all worldly things are impermanent'; and *Chisoku* (知足): 'contentment' or 'being happy with what you have'.

We reached the end of the corridor, where my room stood near the library. The sign outside it said *Tenkū Yume Kagayaku* (天空夢輝), which literally translates as 'dreams sparkling in the celestial sphere'. I took it as a reminder to spend as much time as I could up on the meditation deck while I was there.

Next to the floor-to-ceiling window overlooking the forest was a small desk and chair. The only other furniture was a set of two single beds, each with two half-size tatami mats on top, inspired by the idea that we only need one tatami mat to sleep on and half a mat to sit, meditate and live on.

I had booked onto a workshop with one of Japan's leading yoga teachers, Mako Kataoka. She began by reminding us that yoga is really all about quietening the mind. Indeed, the *Yoga Sutras of Patanjali*, the core text that every yoga teacher studies in training, states '*yogaḥ citta-vṛtti-nirodhaḥ*',[13] meaning that yoga is the stilling of the fluctuations of the mind. The sutras expound that once the mind rests in a state of tranquillity, one can experience life as it is.

As Kataoka-sensei spoke, it dawned on me that the Sanskrit word *citta*, translated into English as 'mind' in a yoga context, is rendered in Japanese as *kokoro*. Later, I would check a host of

Japanese-language yoga training textbooks for confirmation and discover that this was true in every case. Without any detailed knowledge of the original Sanskrit, from studying the sutras in English I had always thought '*yogaḥ citta-vṛtti-nirodhaḥ*' referred only to the stilling of mind chatter, yet here was a whole other dimension of meaning. The stillness sought is a stillness in the whole of our being.

I would also come to notice that the same was true in the case of one of the bestselling Zen books of all time, *Zen Mind, Beginner's Mind* by Sōtō Zen priest Shunryū Suzuki. In the sixties he gave a series of lectures about Zen in English, which were later gathered into the book that birthed the famous quote: 'In the beginner's mind there are many possibilities, but in the expert's there are few.'[14] I sought out the Japanese translation of the book and discovered that throughout the text, other than in the title itself, 'mind' is consistently translated as *kokoro*.

In *Zen Mind, Beginner's Mind*, Suzuki said, 'The mind which is always on your side is not just your mind, it is universal mind, always the same, not different from another's mind. It is Zen mind. It is big, big mind. This mind is whatever you see – this mind is at the same time everything.'[15] This mind is *kokoro*.

Curiously, commenting on this, Zen priest Shōhaku Okumura has said that he believes Suzuki Rōshi was speaking of the meaning of mind, or *kokoro*, as it developed from the Sanskrit term *hrdaya* rather than *citta*.[16] *Hrdaya* is often translated as 'spiritual heart', or that which gives and takes in perfect balance.[17]

Rev. Okumura went on to explain *kokoro*, saying it 'ultimately refers to the entire network of interdependent origination in which we are born, live and die, and to which we awaken through our practice'.[18] Life, in other words.

I am beginning to get the sense that the true meaning of *kokoro* and its bearing on a human life is so much more profound than I ever realised. A place has emerged where languages and cultural perspectives overlap, and I sense that an important truth is hovering. It's not just about quietening the noisy chatter in the head, but also quietening the heart, so it can hear and be heard, and our connection to everything else can be felt and known.

> '**I came to realise clearly that** *kokoro*
> **is nothing other than mountains and**
> **rivers and the great wide earth, the**
> **sun and the moon and the stars.'**
>
> *Zen Master Eihei Dōgen*[19]

Moonbathing

Sitting on the deck at Zenbō Seinei later that evening, I was entranced by a luminous full moon. It looked as if someone had punched a hole in the sky, revealing a silvery light source beyond. Everyone on the retreat sat in meditation chairs in silence, facing out to the distant treeline, waiting.

Tsukimi (月見), or moon-viewing, has been a popular seasonal pastime in Japan for centuries. Back in the Heian period (794–1185 CE), long before the arrival of electricity, aristocrats would hold tea ceremonies and poetry recitals under the moon. In Zen Buddhism, the moon is a symbol of enlightenment. In Japanese mythology, the moon god Tsukuyomi-no-Mikoto is brother of the celestial sun goddess Amaterasu Ōmikami.[20] Some say the moon symbolises the rhythm of time itself, so it is no wonder it has been the muse of poets through the ages.

Under the full moon on Awaji Island that night, I recalled lines by the poet Saigyō, an itinerant monk who lived in twelfth-century Japan. He spoke of how the heart swells with the moon, 'out toward what distant end I know not'.[21]

It was a very special evening. A once-in-a-lifetime astronomical phenomenon was about to take place, as the earth, the sun, the moon and the planet Uranus all fell into alignment. Not only did we witness a total lunar eclipse that night, we experienced a lunar occultation of Uranus by the eclipsed moon. According to the National Astronomical Observatory of Japan, the last time a total lunar eclipse had coincided with a planetary eclipse was in 1580,[22] a time when warlord and military leader Oda Nobunaga was active unifying Japan after years of civil war.[23] Shakespeare was a teenager, and Francis Drake was on his way back to England after circumnavigating the globe on the *Golden Hind*. The next coincidence of lunar eclipse and planetary occultation won't be until 2344, more than three centuries from now,[24] and long after my time on this planet will have come to an end.

There was something about this timeline which struck me like a gong in the dark. What I was witnessing would *never* happen again in my lifetime. I was drawn to give it my full attention, and my eyes did not leave the sky as the moon turned burnt orange and a pin-prick of light passed behind it. A shooting star flew across the sky and I wondered what life might be like if we gave that level of attention to everything we truly care about, aware that this time could be our only time, or our last time, and that we are blessed to witness it. A conversation with a loved one. A fine toasted cheese sandwich. A poem read out loud. A belly laugh with a friend. A sunset. A tear, wiped from a plump cheek. A swim in the sea. An hour alone writing by a steamed-up window in a favourite cafe on a rainy day.

The next morning, we met early for sunrise yoga, rubbed peppermint and eucalyptus balm into our temples, and did a slow barefoot walking meditation up and down the deck as a delicate mist rose over the forest. We finished with a prayer of gratitude that we were there, together, alive in that beautiful place.

I had been at Zenbō Seinei for less than twenty-four hours, but it had felt so much longer than that. Time is such a strange thing. I still carried many of my questions, but knew I could no longer use my precious days simply to track the endless cycle of producing and consuming that society seemed to want for me.

As I packed away my things and prepared to head to the port to journey onwards, I began to wonder whether my question of a life well lived was actually a question of time. Not just a question of linear time as a resource for us to divvy up, sell and spend as efficiently as possible, but time as it relates to the entirety of existence. There was only one way to find out.

KOKORO WORK: STILLNESS

- What everyday activities or occurrences would you savour more if you knew that the next time would be the last time?
- Take a moment to get quiet, breathe deeply and listen from your *kokoro*. What do you need to know today?
- How could you build more opportunities for stillness and silence into your daily life?

KOKORO WISDOM

A life well lived is a life enriched by stillness.

The *kokoro* speaks quietly, in impulses
and feelings. The more often we can find
stillness, the more readily we can tune in to
its wisdom. According to Japanese custom,
peace and quiet can also help cleanse the
kokoro, so light can shine in, and shine out.

CHAPTER 4

TIME

A voice like thunder

A few days later, trying not to trip in a pair of standard-issue lethal plastic slippers, I made my way up a tall flight of polished wooden steps towards the Butsuden, the vast Buddha Hall at the heart of the eight-hundred-year-old monastery known as Eiheiji[1], the Temple of Eternal Peace.

'Go to Eiheiji,' my friend Kazumi had said when I told her of my trip intentions and my midlife malaise. 'It's where I go anytime my *kokoro* needs quiet.'

Eiheiji is spread over a hillside in rural Fukui, and surrounded by a forest of ancient cedar trees. Many of its buildings are joined by a series of long corridors and covered wooden staircases, open at the sides to take in the weather and the surrounding garden. Climbing the stairs, my whole body hurt around the edges, as if someone had outlined me with a marker pen, such was the intensity of the zazen meditation session I had just experienced. Still, what did I expect at Japan's most rigorous Zen temple?

According to Zen priest Dainin Katagiri, who trained at Eiheiji in the sixties, 'Zazen is not a way to escape from life by being mindful of something that is apart from the human world; it is the practice of being present in the real stream of time and looking directly at life itself. Zazen enables you to plunge below the surface and leads you to touch the very core of your life.'[2]

When the session was over, we were invited to explore the temple complex. I had been wandering from one wooden building to another, trying to shake the discomfort from my limbs, paying more attention to my aches than my surroundings. Until, that is, I stepped into the Butsuden and froze, open-mouthed. In all my years of coming to Japan I had never been to Eiheiji before, yet I had a strange sense of déjà vu on entering the Buddha Hall. It only took me a few moments to realise why.

It was the setting for the recurring dream I have had since turning forty, where a man in robes appears before me balancing a sphere of golden light in his hands. He is always positioned in front of three statues, at the back of a cavernous, dark room, just like the one I was in.

The signboard by the doorway told me those statues were of Amida Buddha, the Buddha of the past, Shakyamuni Buddha, the Buddha of the present, and Maitreya Buddha, the Buddha of the future. Only the statue of the present was fully visible. The others were partially hidden from view, as they are in life, and as they always are in my dream.

It was only then that I realised the man who kept showing up in that dream, carrying a golden sphere, was Zen Master Eihei Dōgen, who founded Eiheiji and the Sōtō school of Japanese Zen back in the thirteenth century.

In the dream he always speaks in a low voice, uttering words that I don't understand.

As I stood in the Buddha Hall staring, I heard a whisper: *All you need to know is right here. The rest is commentary.* I didn't understand that either.

Not understanding is a common response to the teachings of this giant of Japanese Zen. I have been attempting to read his work for quarter of a century, since I first stumbled across him in Japanese Studies way back at university and then met him over and over in the intervening years.

Encountering Dōgen

Back in the days I worked in Tokyo, my walk to the nearby underground station from a small apartment near Waseda took me past the unassuming Dairyūji Temple, where a statue of Dōgen and a temple cook drying mushrooms in the midday sun told the story of an important lesson the Zen Master learnt while studying in China.

The story goes that Dōgen asked the elderly man why he was working, given that he was a senior monk who could delegate his tasks and, besides, it was such a hot day. The monk replied that if he didn't do the work himself, he would not have the experience of it, so he would not gain the benefit of the understanding that only comes with experience. He also said that the day's conditions were the right conditions for drying mushrooms. The monk had no idea what the conditions would be like another day – it might rain, it might be cold – so 'now' was the time and he was the person to do it.

I sometimes spent the metro ride to work thinking about the statue and the story, and wondering what this said about the importance of bringing your best effort to every moment, not putting things off or passing them off to other people, because understanding comes from doing. Of course, there are many reasons that this could be seen as bad advice – delegation frees us up and helps others learn, and we simply cannot do everything at once. Curiously, though, these very logical arguments are connected to linear time and how we prioritise ways to be efficient, and in doing so perhaps miss the opportunity of practice here and now.

Later in life, Dōgen would develop this idea into one of his most important teachings: that enlightenment isn't something we work towards and achieve one day in the future but, rather, is something that emerges out of practice as we practise. He called this *shūshō ittō* (修証一等), the oneness of practice and realisation.

I'd ponder this for a while, until I was shaken from my thoughts by the train arriving at Iidabashi station, where I'd alight and rush in high heels alongside thousands of other commuters to catch my connection and head into a long day at the office.

And then there was the time I was sipping tea in the studio of a kimono designer in Kyoto, discussing ephemerality and temporality, when he suddenly sat up and said, 'You should read Dōgen to understand these things.'

Dōgen is perhaps the single most influential teacher in the history of Zen. His core message is simple: life is happening here and now, and each moment is an opportunity to wake up. And yet, the intricacies of his teachings are complex, particularly as they relate to the nature of time. Even native speakers struggle with his ideas, and there exist volumes of translations from Dōgen's original texts into contemporary Japanese, never mind into myriad other languages.

I have read and re-read his notoriously opaque words, and various commentaries on those words. I have taken workshops taught by leading scholars and carried his questions with me on many a walk. On occasion, his voice comes thundering through time to shake me awake when I have been lulled into dullness by the stuff of everyday life. I sit up and listen, and think that I am coming close to an understanding of something I really need to know, but then I try to articulate it and it dissolves. Still, I keep trying, because I know something is there.

Despite this going on for years, it wasn't until this moment at Eiheiji that I made the connection between the words in the books and the man in my dream, to see that it was Dōgen himself, standing in front of the three statues of time there in his own temple, holding a radiant golden sphere. What could it mean? And what did it have to teach me about making the most of this precious life?

Instructions for timefulness

Taking a seat on a bench at the back of the hall, I reached into my backpack and pulled out a commentary on *Uji*, Dōgen's major teaching on the nature of time.[3] *Uji* was written in 1240 when Dōgen was forty years old – the same age I was when I started having the recurring dream about him.

Uji can be found in Dōgen's masterwork *Shōbōgenzō*, which is said to contain some of the most important teachings in all of Zen. Of all the fascicles of *Shōbōgenzō*, *Uji* is the one that has always intrigued me the most. Even the title is curious. It is written 有時, using characters representing the verb 'to be' or 'to exist' (有) and the noun 'time' (時). Under normal circumstances the combination 有時 might be read 'yūji' or 'arutoki' and can variously mean things such as 'at a certain time', 'sometimes', 'once' or 'there is a time', referring to a specific and limited period of time. But the same combination of characters rendered by Dōgen with the reading of 'uji' means something else entirely.

Uji has been translated in many ways by many scholars, but the simplest and perhaps most potent translation is 'being-time'. Another popular version is 'for the time being', which, for Dōgen, encompasses all states of existence-time – the entire universe in a moment. In *Uji*[4], Dōgen says:

An old master named Yaoshan said:
  'For the time being standing on top of the highest peak, just being-time.

For the time being moving along the bottom of the deepest sea, being time.

... In this word "being-time", time is already just being, and all being is time.'

According to this master teaching, existence and time are not separate.

We are time.

Think about this for a minute. We talk about time as a thing, something separate from ourselves that moves like an object: time flies. An hour drags. A decade is gone in a flash. We treat time as something we can spend, waste or negotiate. Make time. Save time. Buy time. Spare time. But what if time and existence are the same thing? What if we are not separate from time?

This is at once immensely complex and beautifully simple. 'Wasting time' becomes wasting our own existence. 'Making time' becomes creating our own life out of what really matters. 'Killing time' is unspeakable. And 'time is money', laughable. Dōgen's teaching makes me question why we so casually give our time away.

This idea of Dōgen's has rattled around in my brain for years, but I have never quite been able to reconcile it with the linear structure of modern life. There, on a quiet hillside in a remote part of Japan, surrounded by bells and prayers and ancient cedars, it was very easy to be calm, to turn my face slowly to the sun and breathe deeply, fully engaged in the moment, imagining myself and time to be one. But I was also very aware that my daily life did not always feel like that.

With two young children to raise, a business to run and books to write, my week is a beautifully scheduled thing. I box it off, day by day, hour by hour, sometimes fifteen minutes by fifteen minutes, comforted by the delusion that I somehow have the power to decide what will unfold in a future that is not yet here. It is efficient, and yet I can't help sensing that I am narrowing my options by scheduling things with quite so much precision.

The day is often diced up instead of flowing with the seasons, the moon, the unfolding of the world. Linear time puts us on high alert for the wrong things. Alarms and notifications and reminders give us a false sense of emergency, to the extent that we get so caught up in our daily doings that we lose sight of the real emergencies of the world.

Society's demands to deliver at speed and under pressure have even spilt over into language. We have to dash off. Catch up. Run an errand. Squeeze something in. The more proficient we get at 'managing time' and the more savvy we get at employing life hacks and shortcuts, the more stuff moves in to fill the boxes on the schedule. It is relentless and endless, and it's simply impossible to do all the things we are called on to do, many of which are out of alignment with what we might actually choose to do if we took the time to prioritise what we really care about most.

Of course it would be hard to function in the modern world without some kind of schedule. How would you know when to put the recycling out, what time to drop the children at school, or when to get to the airport for a flight? How would we get close to dealing with the piled-up to-do lists, have all the meetings, make all the plans? A schedule offers a convenient way to knit our lives together, giving us half a chance of colliding at a particular point in time and space.

Because clock time pervades all aspects of modern life, it is easy to forget that it is simply a clever human construct which fixes a framework to our lives. One might call it 'doing-time'. Perhaps it is no coincidence that the phrase 'doing time' is also English slang for 'being in prison'. There is no doubt linear time can be helpful for functioning in society, but perhaps it is also a distraction from the truth of the eternal now, which sees our lives as a constant flow of arising moments, each one precious and deserving of our full attention.

What if, as Dōgen suggests, there is such a thing as 'being-time', and that we are time-beings – beings made of time – and everything else that exists is a time-being too? What if each moment contains all the being-time of all time-beings – the past, the present, the future, all possibility, everything arising at once?

This is what Dōgen seems to be saying, and it aligns perfectly with what one learned Japanese gentleman, a different Mr Tsuji, told me when I asked him where the *kokoro* is located. His response sent me reeling. He said, '*Kokoro* exists in time. Without time there is no *kokoro*.' And here is Dōgen saying that without time there is no us. To me, this feels like a whole new way to look at life, and death.

Taking care of now

My head hurt from all the thinking, so I set off in search of a cup of tea. At Hakujukan[5], the lodge next to Eiheiji, I encountered a friendly nun with a kind, open face. I asked her a question, and we fell into easy conversation.

She confirmed that *Shōbōgenzō* is a kind of cosmology, a metaphysical study of the nature of the universe exploring 'time' beyond the scope of what most of us can comprehend, and that even though it was written in a different era, it is just as relevant today.

The nun gently cautioned me, 'When studying Dōgen you have to remember that he is not talking about the minute by minute scheduling of time that creates the illusion of this world of speed. He is talking about the vastness of time – the scope of a human lifespan, which is at once minuscule and unimaginably huge.'

Dōgen wrote that there are 6,400,099,980 moments in a day.[6] No one seems to know where he got that figure from, but it makes the point that a moment is infinitesimally small. He said sixty-five moments arise and disappear in the space of a finger snap,[7] each moment over almost before it has begun. The actual duration is less important than the fact that it illustrates Dōgen's 'moment' not as a span of time we can intellectually grasp, but one so short that in living it, we experience 'time' as something that flows in us, as we flow as it.

Theoretical physicist Carlo Rovelli, writing eight hundred years after Dōgen, has put it this way: 'If by "time" we mean nothing more than happening, then everything is time. There is *only* that which exists in time.'[8]

The nun was a similar age to me, and I explained why I was there, and how I was seeking answers to questions about how to live so when I get to the end of my life and look back, I will know I lived it well.

Smiling, she said, 'If you take care of the present moment, and give the now your full attention, it connects to both past and future. You can see that everything now has been born from the past, and everything now connects to the future. So, your job is to take care of now, as well as you can.'

The nun told me of her life before taking her vows, back when she had long hair and cute shoes. She said things were a lot easier now she was walking this path of sufficiency and contentment. She was no longer consumed by a lust for stuff, and her life was not a product of what she owned or did not own. There was not a line on her face, and when she laughed, which she did often, she seemed to glow.

I asked her how she made the decision to become a nun and she simply said, 'It was time.'

'But how do you know when it's time for something so significant?' I asked.

'Follow the threads of connection,' she counselled. 'Be where you have to be. Don't force the answers. They will arrive, and you will know.'

The heartbeat of the world

As night drew in around the Temple of Eternal Peace, I lay back on my bed and picked up my copy of *Uji* again. It opened at the part which begins 'As the time right now is all there ever is, each being-time is without exception entire time.'[9] I kept reading until I fell asleep.

Just a few hours later, I woke at 3.30 a.m. to wash my face, get dressed and join some thirty others for a short lecture ahead of *asa no otsutome*, the dawn prayers and sutra reading undertaken by the monks of Eiheiji each morning in the Dharma Hall, at the highest point of the monastery. I was given a concertina booklet of sutras and advised that I must not take it into the toilet, drop it or sit on it. My hands were suddenly sweaty, and I was convinced I would accidentally do all of those things.

We were ushered in silence to the back of the hall, where we took our places, wrapped coats and blankets around our knees against the cold, and waited. Lions guarded an enormous dark altar at the back of the room. A gong sounded. And again, and again. Each strike sent ripples out across the tatami floor.

The booming loudened, and the distance between gong strikes shortened, until the hall was filled with a sound like a huge sheet of metal being flexed, ripples smashing against each other in the air, colliding in my ears and reverberating right through my body.

Monks in ochre and black robes filed in and took their places beneath cascading golden decorations, illuminated by the most gentle of dawn light.

A higher pitched sound, from a singing bowl perhaps, began to alternate with the gong. This strange and beautiful music got faster and faster, crashing over the floor of the Dharma Hall like an avalanche barrelling down a mountain.

And then suddenly, silence.

I felt as if I had just witnessed some kind of invocation of the spirit of Dōgen, whose ashes were housed in the mausoleum next door.

A drum beat, the gong sounded again, and then the monks started to chant the Heart Sutra, all hitting one note so low they sounded like a swarm of bees. I thought about how this happens every morning, as it has for hundreds of years, the monks showing up to pray for all beings, whether or not we are aware of it.

Soon it was the turn of a senior monk to chant alone, in a tone lower than any I have heard in a human voice. Then more group chanting. An insect bite appeared on my left hand and made my ring finger swell so fast I had to remove my wedding ring. It felt like some kind of test. Could I stay focused on the moment, even as the bite called for attention?

Then a gong was struck twice. I looked to one side where a monk was standing by a huge drum, and time began to slow. He drew back the drum stick and with intense concentration struck the taut skin. Between drawback and strike, ten minutes could have passed, or two seconds, or an eternity. I had no idea. All I knew was that in that moment, even as I was in it, the experience was changing me somehow. It was as if Dōgen was expressing his ideas right there, demonstrating the vastness of an infinitesimally short moment within the beat of a drum.

It felt like I had just been given a glimpse of a radical idea, which had been hiding in plain sight for eight hundred years:

> **Unfolding time is a pulsating of energy, the heartbeat of the world, and we exist within its rhythm.**

I found myself coming back to the idea of heart-mindfulness, and the ability to tune in to the intelligence of a moment, and recognise that it contains all of the past and all the potential of the future, here and now, offering a new beginning now and now and now. When we are heart-mindful we act from inside the moment, rather than observing it from the outside. Even as I write this I can see the limitations of language, and sense how I am trying to articulate something which feels right at the edges of what my conscious brain can grasp, and yet I know that when I pay attention in this way, I feel completely different about this moment, this day, this experience we call life.

Making space

My mind wandered back to Hagurosan, and a conversation I had with one of the holiest men in Japan shortly after climbing the mountain. Master Hoshino is a thirteenth-generation *yamabushi* whose family have worshipped on Dewa Sanzan for centuries. It took me months to arrange an interview with him, only to discover that the man who had been my boss at the Yamagata Prefectural Government a quarter of a century earlier had been in Master Hoshino's class at primary school. It was not the first time I had the feeling that my younger self had laid a trail of connections for me to follow later on, and that later was now.

Part way through the interview I blurted out a question I hadn't been planning to ask: 'What is prayer?'

'Life is prayer,' he said. 'The way we live is the prayer we offer.'

I recalled how Hagurosan is known as the mountain of the present and earthly desires, and thought about how the original term that is often rendered into English as 'earthly desires' is a curious one. *Genzeriyaku* (現世利益) means to receive benefits such as health and good fortune as a reward for an active faith, although monks would tell you that the focus should be the active faith, not any kind of reward. But the literal translation of *genzeriyaku* is 'profits from this world'[10] which, these days, are readily associated with the accumulation of money and status. These kinds of desires can be so damaging to our planet, our communities and our own wellbeing – and, of course, in Buddhism desire is said to be at the root of suffering. Speaking the phrase 'present and earthly desires' aloud to myself also felt like an irony when considered from a material perspective, given that desires are entirely focused on things we don't yet have, and thus pull our attention away from the present into an imaginary future, or sideways into the jet stream of someone else's life, where the comparison begins.

But then it dawned on me:

> The point of prayer in any form is not to ask for what we want, but to offer thanks for what we already have.

Perhaps the real lesson from Hagurosan was about learning to be more active in our faith whatever we believe in – whether our religion has a name, or whether our religion is something else entirely, nature or beauty or art perhaps – thereby infusing each day with a sense of sacredness.

At the top of Hagurosan there is a pool known as Kagami Ike, the mirror pond, where hundreds of Heian-period bronze mirrors have been found, dating back more than a thousand years. In the Shintō tradition mirrors are thought to be objects of near magical potency, and examples of recovered Haguro mirrors are kept in the British Museum in London and the Metropolitan Museum in New York. There is something incredibly freeing about the idea of tossing a mirror into a deep pond, releasing the need to own a physical object in order to see yourself.

I was beginning to sense that midlife could be an opportunity to stop looking outside myself for validation and confirmation of the value of my existence. It was a chance to stop worrying so much about things I don't actually care about, and an important moment to really tune in to how I felt about each aspect of my life so I could prioritise what really mattered.

Spending time in nature, in meditation and in reflection had helped me tune out the noise in my head and tune in to the wisdom of my *kokoro*, which was telling me to slow down further and keep on listening. Instead of being guided by rational decision-making that is based on experiences from the past or an anticipated yet unknowable future, we can be guided by the energy that moves us in the present.

Perhaps it is quite simple, really. We just have to tune in, and approach life heart-mindfully. The more we pay attention to our lives and the more we open to all the options flowing to us – in words, images and feelings – the more sure we can be about what our *kokoro* wants us to know.

A cold wind began to blow and I could sense that winter was on its way. It was time to head home to England. I was on the cusp of understanding something important, and while I couldn't yet fully articulate it, I knew it was connected to the strong urge I felt to carve out some time and space in my life. For years I had leapt from one project to the next, from one deadline to the next, with barely a moment to take stock and sense what was bubbling deep beneath the surface.

I had a growing feeling that I should completely clear my calendar for a substantial period of time, and allow myself to be a bit less visible for a while. As a self-employed business owner this made me incredibly nervous, but I wanted to trust this feeling.

Lisa's words still haunted me: 'If no miracle comes, I'll know. If a miracle comes, I'm going to live fully. Either way, it will be the end of this particular time.' In honour of my late friend, and in recognition that those of us left are the lucky ones, I made a decision there and then to intentionally end my era of endless chasing, and instead to live fully, which began with stepping off the project treadmill for a while. I wasn't giving up; I was simply giving in to the internal call for a life reset.

I made the decision to honour my existing teaching commitments until the end of winter and then enter spring with almost nothing in the calendar. It was the first time in a decade that I had cancelled my plans in one fell swoop. I thought the reason I needed space was to invite in new ideas, which often lead to new opportunities and which would eventually justify the space.

I was quite proud of myself. It felt good. I was buoyant. I thought that with this, my midlife malaise had been sufficiently tended to, and my questions were on the way to being answered.

I could not have been more wrong.

Little did I know that as winter gave way to spring I would need the space for something else entirely, as my mother was handed a terminal cancer diagnosis, and all the questions changed.

KOKORO WORK: TIME

- What is your relationship with time?
- To what extent do you try to plan and control your life? What might be different if you eased up and focused your attention on the present – this point in your life, this week, this day, this hour, this moment?
- What really matters to you right now?

心

KOKORO WISDOM

A life well lived is a life we are present to.

When we spend our days ruminating about the
past or worrying about the future, we are missing
the experience of life as it is unfolding. Our *kokoro*
responds to the world as it is arising in this moment,
so to tune in to the wisdom of the *kokoro*, we need
to stay present to what is right here, right now.

月山

PART TWO: GASSAN

In the shadow of death on Moon Mountain

If you are brave enough to speak of death, you might hear a whispered response from the sacred mountain where ancestral spirits are said to gather. It is a strange and beautiful place, with an alpine meadow so breathtaking they call it Midagahara, the Field of Amida, the Buddha of Infinite Light, and say it is the closest place to the Pure Land – heaven – on earth.

If you are braver still and choose to go there, and climb to the top following the footsteps of a mountain ascetic, you will enter another world where a swirling mist engulfs you like the breath of the spirits themselves.

You will find yourself, and lose yourself, on Gassan, the one they call Moon Mountain.

The tallest of the three sacred mountains of Dewa Sanzan, Gassan (lit. 'Moon Mountain') is said to represent death and the past. This is where our story leads us next, as we learn what the presence of death can teach us about living well.

CHAPTER 5

MORTALITY

Here. Not here.

S itting in the old tartan armchair in my writing room, I was searching for the perfect poem. 'Pick something beautiful,' my mum had said. I reached for the anthology *Finding the Way Home* and it fell open at a short verse by Ōtagaki Rengetsu, a nun, potter and poet who was born more than two centuries ago, but captured human life in a timeless way. Rengetsu, whose name means 'Lotus Moon', lived a tragic yet beauty-filled life. Her poem spoke of the way we accept the graceful falling of mountain cherry blossoms so much more easily than we let go of our attachment to the world.[1]

It was my forty-sixth birthday. The night before, there had been a full moon and a penumbral lunar eclipse. Later that day, our nation would see the coronation of a new king. But all of that seemed unimportant as I sat by the window in the dawn light, thinking about how, in three days' time, I would be hosting my own mother's funeral.

It had all happened so quickly.

My mum had been having difficulty eating for a while. She had been given acid reflux tablets and assured it was nothing serious, but when things did not improve she was sent for an endoscopy. They found a small lump so they did a biopsy. 'A shock but we are optimistic,' Mum texted. She went for a scan, and when the hospital suggested she bring one of her children to get the results, my blood turned to ice. She had oesophageal cancer, but they did not know the extent of it and needed further scans to find out.

We went to a cafe that day and caught up on this and that as we always did. I was determined not to think about the fact that it could be the last time we would go to a cafe together. (It was.) My heart was not ready for those kinds of thoughts. But then she asked me to help her choose some writing paper so she could write letters to friends and family, and I understood that she knew, deep down, what was coming.

Mother's Day

The day after her triple MRI, my parents joined the rest of our family at a rented house which we had strung wall-to-wall with photo bunting, capturing moments from her life. We decorated with fairy lights, toasted Mum at dinner and laughed until we cried over a family quiz, all the while pretending that we weren't doing it to say goodbye. In the day, I was upbeat and practical. At night, I cried until my body felt like a melon with all its seeds scooped out.

That Sunday was March 19, Mother's Day. I had ordered a dried flower wreath as her gift, and as she unboxed it I had a flash forward of me taking it down from her house and bringing it back to mine. I was wearing a summer dress. I shook the image away.

A friend had lent us a beach hut and we spent the day by the sea, Mum wrapped in blankets, drinking in every moment of her grandchildren's laughter. We drew pictures on stones with paint pens and ate fish and chips while seagulls hovered. It was only when everyone else had gone home that Mum sat on the sofa in our lounge looking shattered, asking for a hot water bottle for her back, and saying, 'I want more Christmases, and more birthdays, but then we always want more. How many is enough?' However many we have had, I thought, is not enough.

The next day, my parents stayed long enough to see our

children off to school. Mum stood at the back door waving as Mr K slowly drove off. A moment later, he began to reverse. At first I thought one of the girls had forgotten something, but then I realised, he's giving them one more chance for an imprint of each other. She waved again, and in the flutter of her bony hand I sensed all the words she had no time left to say.

Reflecting on a life

On rainy days when I was little, Mum would go to the cupboard under the stairs, reach through the winter coats and pull out a black bin bag. It was full of books wrapped like gifts, a lucky dip with stories for a prize. Every room in the house had a bookshelf and we spent many happy hours at the library.

Later, when I was getting ready to head off to university to study Japanese, she came with me to London, even though she was scared of the underground. We spent hours in the Japan Centre bookshop, gathering everything on my reading list and sharing the excitement of a new beginning.

A few years ago, she spotted a woman holding a copy of *Wabi Sabi* in Waterstones, considering whether to buy it. Mum later relayed how she had blurted out, 'My daughter wrote that book!' And then had no idea what to say next. I hope she knew that the book in the woman's hands only existed because of the love of words she had instilled in me from a young age.

When I was living with a homestay family in Kyoto as a teenager, calling someone else *Okāsan* (Mother) and struggling with homesickness and overwhelm, she wrote to me and said, 'You are so brave, and adventurous. I don't know where you get it from. You are living a life I would never have dared to live, but would have loved to. Keep going.'

I soaked in those words, and for many years believed that I was indeed braver than her, until those final days when I realised her bravery in friendship, in love and in suffering far outshone mine.

Although my mum saw the good in everyone and everything, like most people who have experienced difficulty she carried regret and worry for much of her life. But something shifted the day she got her diagnosis. It was as if she realised in that moment that the heavy things she carried were rocks stitched into the lining of a coat she had been choosing to wear. On the way out of the consultant's office she took it off and handed it over saying, *I won't be needing this any more.*

There was an acceptance evident in her right from that moment. *Well, this is how it is, so let's make the most of what time we have left together.* I kept waiting for her upbeat words to be swept aside by anger, or resentment, or a sense of unfairness, but it never happened. Although there were moments of utter sadness for all the things she would miss, there was also a wholly unexpected lightness about her. This woman, who had spent much of her life ruminating about the past or worrying about the future, was suddenly and almost completely focused on the present. As a result, while the three remaining weeks we had with her were devastating in their brevity, they were also precious, beautiful and deeply inspiring in a way I am only just beginning to understand.

'I am not afraid,' she told me categorically a few days before she died, and I wondered what it was about the way she had lived, or had chosen to face death, which made her so clear about that.

The truth was, I was afraid. I was terrified of being swallowed up by the gaping hole I knew she would leave behind, which was edging closer by the day. I was afraid of feeling alone. There was no one other than Mr K who was interested in me in the way she had always been. I realised that I was a complete beginner at this.

I had never lost my mother before. I had never even been at the side of a dying person before. I had never seen a dead body before.

My phone buzzed with a message from a friend in Tokyo: 'This is probably the most important work you will ever do, as a child, for your mother.'

I didn't know if I could do it, yet I knew that I absolutely would.

Time, slipping away

A couple of days later I took a train back to my parents' house to help Mum with paperwork. We were in her study, surrounded by folders and half-drunk cups of tea, when her phone rang. Mum had an appointment with the consultant the following Monday to get her results, and was not expecting the call. She was certainly not expecting to be told there and then that there was nothing they could do. It was only by chance I had been with her when the call came. I did not recognise the sound that left my body.

She decided to keep it from everyone else in our family until the weekend, to give herself some time to process the news before it was weighed down with everyone else's sorrow. She swore me to secrecy, and sent me home with a list of things to do, insisting that I didn't miss the girls' school play the following day. Sitting in the village hall, watching them sing songs about pirates and mermaids, all I could think of was my mum at her desk writing goodbyes to her friends and figuring out a way to tell my two brothers and our dad.

The following Monday, the consultant looked her in the eye and confirmed what she already knew: 'You have terminal cancer. It's spread from your oesophagus into your bones. It's in your spine, your neck, your jaw, your hip.'

My mother declined palliative chemo, and instead had what

should have been a routine procedure, to put in a stent where her oesophagus met her stomach to help her eat. With luck we would have her for another three to six months, they said. But the wire mesh slipped, and after a night of vomiting, she was in terrible pain and rushed to hospital in an ambulance. They repositioned the stent the following day, but it was too late. She barely ate again. I had packed for one night, but ended up staying until she died in a hospice less than three weeks later.

The hospice was calmer than the hospital. Even though the days themselves were numbered, each one felt vast and unhurried. Unable to eat, Mum was losing weight rapidly. We made a rota for visitors and each one was a joy, but drained her so much we soon had to switch to family only, and invited messages by text instead. I read them aloud to her one by one. *I love you. I love you. I love you.*

The photo bunting from Mother's Day was strung up around the bed and her room was filled with flowers. One of the nurses, smiling at a photo of Mum and her youngest grandson in huge shades and fake fur coats courtesy of a Snapchat filter, commented, 'I think the meaning of life is to get to the end having been loved, and everyone you love knowing that you loved them.'

'I absolutely agree,' my mum replied.

'I think you are so brave, you know,' the nurse said.

'Brave? Me? Why?' Mum asked.

'I've seen you two working on those letters, day after day. How many have you written now?'

'Fifty-six,' she said, beaming at me.

'It's such a brave thing to be so honest about what is happening, and to write it over and over on paper so that you can say goodbye. And it is so selfless of you to focus on others at a time like this.'

'Oh, I think doing things for other people is the best way

to deal with hard things,' said my mum, sounding like a good Buddhist. 'To be honest, they are as much for me as for them. My friends have brought me so much joy, and reminding them of that has brought me joy all over again.'

Then she turned to me. 'What was it that nun said again?' She was remembering a documentary I had told her about, featuring the Japanese nun, novelist and activist Jakuchō Setouchi, who lived her life to the fullest right up until she died aged ninety-nine.

'To live is to love.'

The world carried on, but we had no idea about it. I was determined not to lose what little time we had left to anticipatory grief. I wrote things down, spoke thoughts into my phone, took photos and videos, asked questions, and sat for hours just watching my mother sleep, as if to drink her in before she vanished, along with all notions of a future with her in it.

That evening, as one of the hospice staff took her off for a bath, she turned, looked me in the eye and said, 'Thank you for everything.' I wasn't ready for a final goodbye so I said, 'We have our special day tomorrow. Just you and me. Do you promise you will be bright and breezy?' She promised and the orderly wheeled her out of the room.

I gathered up my things and left for the evening, passing the bathroom on my way out. The door was shut, and her wheelchair stood outside, empty.

Waiting

A couple of days later, she was moved into a private room. No one needed tell us it was where people went to die. The room was big enough for a couple of rollout beds and had doors facing the garden, so we decided that at least one of us would be with Mum around the clock. She did not want to be alone, and we did not want to leave her side. That meant we caught every extraordinary word she uttered.

Mum said she could see a group of children lined up like a chain of paper people, all looking like my younger brother. She saw my husband on a mountain. She saw a little girl with a gold coin, which she wanted 'to put on the wall with all the rest'. She asked us, 'What's in the box? It helps people.' And she declared that, 'All the family is in a line holding hands, Grandma, Grandad, husband, children and partners, grandchildren all together.'

Another day, she said, 'I've sat myself down on a rock', staring ahead as if she was gazing out to sea. She looked comfortable and content. Speaking took effort, but she said it again to make sure we heard her. My family all live by the sea at various points along the south coast of England, and it felt like an invitation to go in search of her near the waves.

She was clearly in some in-between place, moving between here and there, wherever 'there' was. She talked of abstract things like light and shapes, as well as concrete things like huge rooms full of people and strings of lanterns lighting the way. Another day, she spoke of being in a queue. There were many, many people lining up beneath a flickering list of names, like an old-fashioned airport departure board.

Each day she would rally for a few hours, get woozy at night and fall into a deep sleep. We would think we were losing her and then she would wake at dawn to the sound of the birds, sit up and say, 'Good morning', with absolute delight. There is an enchanting phrase in Japanese, *kokoro ni kizamu*, which means to inscribe something on your heart. That is what I did with the words we repeated to each other each morning:

We get to have this day.

We gave her spa treatments. We played jazz, or listened to the rain, shared stories, and sometimes shared silence. At one point, she looked around at us, her gathered family, and said, 'I am just so happy. Sometimes life has been hard but I wouldn't change anything, because it has led me here surrounded by all this love. What more could I want?'

'Push me into the garden,' she said. 'Oh, it couldn't be more lovely. Let's make a video.' And then, looking around in wonder, 'I'm living on the right side of life.'

I remember the sun that day. It shone right out of her.

Sometimes it was brutal. She was sick and I didn't know how to help her. She was as thin as a twig, and I couldn't feed her. She was fully aware of all the things she would never experience again, and I couldn't tell her she was wrong. But then, so often, she was bright, full of stories and laughter, clearly nourished by the flood of love from friends and family. We took it in turns to keep an overnight vigil, and stretching out on my yoga mat in the depths of night, I was deeply aware that we were at the opening of a portal. I could sense sorrow hovering at the edges but was glad that we were still in the before, together.

Since long ago, there has been a tradition in Japan for poets, warriors and Zen monks to write death poems. As I lay in the dark, a swirl of words by samurai Date Masamune danced like dust motes through the shaft of light which fell across her bed:

'I survived the darkness of this fleeting world guided only by the bright moon in my heart.'[2]

I pondered what it must be like to contemplate your own

death, not in an abstract 'some day' kind of way, but in a very real 'perhaps today' kind of way. Looking back, I wonder why even then, with death at the door, I was considering it as if it were something that only happens to other people.

Thinking about this now, I recall how Naoki-san once told me that Japanese culture is all about death, and he was not the first person to tell me that. It is there in the lament of seasonal poetry, in the painted petals of falling cherry blossom, and in the traditions of honouring ancestors as part of the community. An awareness of death is an awareness of impermanence, known in Japanese as *mujyō* (無常). I thought I already lived with such an awareness, but as my mother faded away I realised that until that point my understanding had only been intellectual. It was only when all kinds of age-related endings were colliding with the imminent loss of my mother, that I really understood what it meant, and how important it is to cultivate a strong sense of what really matters, so we can treasure it before it is lost, and make the most of every day.

On the morning of the day before she died, lying on her side she seemed smaller somehow. Her cheeks were caving in, her face darkened around the eye sockets, hinting at the skull beneath. All padding had fallen away. Her shoulders, in purple pyjamas, were moving up and down slowly. Her hands were warm and her face relaxed, but she seemed to be waiting for something. Mr K was bringing the girls that day, the last of the grandchildren to visit. I wondered if she was waiting for one more dose of joy.

Mum had been a huge part of the girls' lives since they were born, taking care of them when Mr K and I had to work. She was their first friend and they loved her like a favourite teddy. They showed up with their best clothes on, a little nervous, not knowing what to expect, but as happy to see Grandma as she was to see them.

There was chit-chat and laughter and gentle hugs, and then Mum drifted off to sleep. The girls made a video, which I showed her afterwards when she realised they had gone.

She asked, 'How did it end?'

'This is how it ended,' I said, showing her their sweet faces in the small screen of my phone as they leant over and told her how much they loved her.

'Just wonderful,' she whispered. Time seemed to bounce back and forwards, what seemed true one minute unfathomable the next.

The night before she died I gave her a bath. A clever contraption lifted her tired body from wheelchair to tub, I put on some meditation music and she lay back, finally letting go of all her tension. She no longer cared that she was a skeleton with skin, and relaxed against the wall of the tub. For the next thirty minutes I poured warm water over her, watched it pool around the sharp bones of her clavicles, and listened as she talked of how blissful the bath was and how grateful she was for everything.

Endings, beginnings

If you asked me to describe my mum's death I could speak of the moment of her passing, the sheer physicality of it, where her extremities went cold, her eye sockets darkened, her wrinkles seemed to fall away from her face, and her breathing simply slowed and then stopped. Or I could recount the death poem of Chine, sister of one of Matsuo Bashō's disciples: 'It lights up / as swiftly as it fades: / a firefly.'[3]

Or I could speak of the hours before her passing, when we

gathered round her bed, where she lay with her hands folded over her heart, and my older brother read from *The Enchanted Wood*. I could tell you how we took it in turns to hold her hand and stroke her hair, or how I quietly sang 'When You Need Me'. Or I could tell you how I whispered of her bravery and our love for her, how it was okay for her to go, and that I would look for her in the wind and the waves and the stars and the rain, having no idea where the words were coming from.

I could tell you how she sighed, 'I'm out of time, aren't I?' and then turned to us and said, with effort and determination, uttering one syllable on each breath, 'I-will-al-ways-love-you-all.' Her death poem, spoken out loud.

Or I could speak of the moment she passed, when I suddenly felt my chest filled with a particular kind of light, not a weightless gentle glow as you might imagine from a candle, but a dense and heavy light. I remember once reading that a tablespoon of neutron star weighs more than a billion tons if you bring it to earth. It was like that. Dense starlight, the weight of a mountain, floating in my chest, occupying all the space from the heart centre up to my clavicles at the front of my body, just beneath the skin.

I wondered if it was a fraction of her life force, or whether it was all the light she had stored up to beam at me and my children in the future, which she was depositing in advance, for us to draw on whenever we needed it. I can still feel it now. Even as the rest of my body has experienced everything grief can throw at it, from shaking and shivering, to nausea and numbness, the dense starlight has remained.

My mother died on 15 April, in the peak of spring, as the cherry tree in my garden sent its petals floating to the ground, where they would remain until I returned home to my children the following day, and to the realisation that I had absolutely no idea how to live in a world without her in it.

Silent spring

The days that followed were grey and moody, or sunny but cold. I spent a lot of time at my desk, making practical arrangements and doing sadmin. When I could no longer stand telling yet another stranger that my mother had died, I would pull on my old brown boots and head up the river, picking my way carefully to avoid crushing bright celandines underfoot.

One afternoon in early May, I was weeding the rose garden while my youngest daughter was sitting on the swing seat, eating cucumber and looking out for butterflies.

'When does Grandma get shredded?' Maia asked casually, as if checking what time her train got in.

'Oh, sweet girl, she gets cremated next week. Cremated means turned to ashes so we can scatter her somewhere beautiful.'

'Like in a garden to help the flowers grow?'

'Yes, exactly. Grandma wanted her ashes scattered in a bluebell wood.'

'So if we go there, will we be able to see her face on the bark of a tree?'

'Wouldn't that be wonderful,' I said, half-hoping.

A few days later, I turned forty-six. There was, of course, no phone call from my mum, no surprise visit, no thoughtfully chosen gift. But the thing that struck me most was the absence of her handwriting. Never again would she write my name.

I went for a swim in the sea. It was unseasonably cold and

huge waves bashed me about. Worried that I would lose my rings in the water, I used the thumb of my left hand to hold them in place. There was a third band there now, my grandmother's wedding ring, passed to me just a few weeks before. Salty water crashed over my body and poured down my face. Waves. Tears. Audacious aliveness.

I watched the waves crash against dark rocks, and searched for my mother but could not find her there. I tracked a seagull skating on the thermals, wings wide and strong, and I listened to the water rolling in, rolling on.

Life was the shape of an eye, emerging from nothing, full in the middle with love and laughter, fear and disappointment, hope and dreams, and then returning to nothing. For a moment I thought I saw that eye as part of a face, a body in a setting, laid out across the sea, and I saw everything in the context of everything else. I saw where the light comes from, and how the life we glimpse is but a tiny inkling of a bigger picture we cannot fathom.

And then I felt very cold.

Oh my god she died. My mother *died*. My *mother* died.

I could rely on her for absolutely anything, except to not do that.

KOKORO WORK: MORTALITY

Please go gently with these questions and, if you need to, talk to someone as you explore them.

- Take the three-week test. If you knew that the next three weeks would be your last – that you would be fine and healthy and then just gone – how would you spend that

time? What does that say about your priorities? Are there any actions you need to take right now, just in case?
- What do you hope happens when we die?
- Have a conversation about death or endings with someone. After your conversation, note down any observations of what was said and how it made you feel to talk about it.

KOKORO WISDOM

A life well lived is a life lived in full awareness of the impermanence of everything.

One of the devastating truths about being human is that we will eventually lose everyone and everything that we truly care about. When we are attuned to the *kokoro*, the storehouse of our feelings and emotions, we can cultivate a strong sense of what matters most, so we can treasure it before it is lost, and make the most of every day.

CHAPTER 6

FALLING

Letting go. Being carried.

When I was growing up I had no vocabulary for death. I have lost all my grandparents and their siblings, an aunt, a cousin, college dorm mates, work colleagues and family friends to illnesses, accidents and old age, yet while I acutely remember the ache of each loss, I have few memories of talking about any of them. Perhaps because of this, as I got older I became superstitious, thinking that to speak of death and grief would invite them in, even though they had already arrived, without invitation. But the black hole which swallowed my mother was so huge I could not possibly have hidden it from our daily lives, even if I had wanted to, which I did not.

Not long after she died, I had a chat about death with our nine-year-old while making pancakes one Sunday morning. I surprised myself with my openness, and realised that as my mother departed this world, something in me had cracked. Light had been pouring in, in a most unexpected way, and I wanted to share that in my conversation with my daughter, so the darkness was not all she remembered.

'Mummy, don't say "dead",' Sienna said.

'Why not?' I asked, fearing that she had inherited my superstition.

'Because "dead" means "ended" and Grandma is not ended.'

Grandma is not ended. Those words would swirl in my head and heart for months, as I tried to figure out where she had gone, and whether our lives really do have some kind of continuum, or whether this is it and then it's over.

Every religion in the world has something to say about what happens when we die, much of it conflicting. I had no idea what I believed. My brain was a jumble of theories about the afterlife (including whether or not there is one), memories of her words in those final days, and my felt experience of the moment she passed. And if the coin had death on one side, of course it had life on the other. My midlife quest had a new question: what could an acute awareness of death teach me about life, and living it well?

There are several words in Japanese for grief including *hitsū* (悲痛), a profound sorrow, *aiseki* 哀惜, the particular sadness of bereavement, and *shūshō* (愁傷), a poetic term that combines 'autumn' and '*kokoro*' with 'wound'. Most words for grief include the heart radical 心 as a foundational element of one of the characters. The term *shōshin* (傷心) literally means 'scarred *kokoro*'.

Grief is the work of the *kokoro*.
The *kokoro* is the beating heart of grief.

After our chat about death my nine-year-old sent me a letter. It said, 'I love you. I know you are sad. I'm always here for you. Come and find me if you ever want a hug or chocolate. I thought that maybe when you're sad but don't want to cry you could draw whatever comes to you.' She had drawn two boxes below the words. She had filled the left-hand box with abstract patterns and a school of fish, and left the other for me to fill in. 'Do it with your eyes closed and just feel it,' she wrote. Little did she know that was exactly how I was navigating grief.

In the centre of the shadow

I was untethered, floating, with nothing to hold on to, and with nothing holding on to me. It was grief, I knew, and yet I also knew it was not just grief. I was simultaneously experiencing an involuntary shedding of what I realised I no longer needed or cared about, and a death-initiated decimation of the very sense of who I was. It was profoundly unsettling. Something told me it would, ultimately, be freeing, but I didn't feel that yet. I just felt like I was drifting, carried on the wind like a sound from far away. I could hear what was going on around me, and a blurred version of myself was participating, but I was not fully there. It was as if the logical, rational part of me had dissolved and I was moving under a different force.

At first, I inhaled books about grief. Memoirs, advice books, novels. But the way they described it was not what I was feeling. I appreciated the writing, and the effort, but after a while I stopped reading. I would be okay for a bit, and then I would remember that my mother was dead. Every time, it sliced like a razor catching on my knee.

I let myself be okay with not wanting to be sociable, with going for a run but ending up lying on the ground, staring up at the sky; with going to bed early in response to the heavy tiredness that descended as the sun went down, so I could wake in time for a sunrise that she would never get to see, and spill ink and tears onto paper.

There is a Japanese term *chūin* (中陰), the bardo, which refers to a period of intermediate existence between one's death and rebirth, believed in Buddhist traditions to last for forty-nine days. I remember a friend telling me that her mother, who was from a very traditional Japanese family, taught her to light an incense stick every day for forty-nine days when someone passed away, because she believed the spirit might feel lost and unsure about leaving. 'We would sit in front of the incense stick and in our minds we would talk to the person who had passed away,' she told me. 'We would let them know that everything was fine here, that they could go.'

According to the calendar, my mother was there in the bardo, and I felt that in some ways I was too. My existence as someone with a living mother in the world had ended the moment she died, and I was in a transition stage, as yet unsure of how or who to be now. I took the word apart in my mind. Of the two characters which combine to make *chūin*, 中 means inside, and 陰 means yin or shadow. I was drifting through the centre of the shadow her absence had cast over our lives. I lit a candle for her, for me, for us, every day for those forty-nine days, just in case.

I was curious about the way all of this had rendered me utterly uninterested in hustling for anything. I had lost all sense of materialism. If I went to the shops, which was rare, I wandered around in a daze and came home empty-handed.

I got the urge to have a big clear-out, and when I was tidying my office I found my journal from a couple of weeks before Mum's diagnosis. I had done an oracle card reading and written it down. I don't associate oracle cards with any particular belief system. Rather, I find them a simple way to connect to what I already know deep down. It's like reading pages that have fluttered out from the book of my *kokoro*.

The card I had pulled before the storm hit said that a turbulent time was coming, but the less I resisted it, the happier I would eventually be. It also said the things I am most attached to would go first, and I must let those things go. 'You will be reminded of your own mortality, and see more clearly where your destiny intersects with those of others,' my notes said. 'Don't push harder.

Instead, slow down and ask the questions that most people don't ask. This place of temporary non-action is meant to be.'

Mr K and I decided to spend the afternoon at the beach. We lay on the pebbles and stared at the sky, the bluest of blues. A seagull flew overhead. We took a selfie and I noticed that the furrow by my right eyebrow had deepened, and it now had a cousin by my left one – and I was surprised how little I cared. A man in a dark jumper was waving a metal detector near the shoreline. I kept waiting for him to bend over and pick up something shiny but his beeper never sounded. The waves rolled in and in. We sat up and scouted about for pebbles.

'Which ones do you like best?' I asked.

'It's hard to see past the white ones,' he said.

And right then I saw a perfect heart-shaped white pebble by my foot. It was smooth to the touch and I put it in my pocket, sneaking it away so the metal detector man wouldn't feel jealous of my treasure.

I kept thinking about the reading. *Ask the questions that most people don't ask.* What was I learning from this most hideous of lessons?

Burning

I'm walking across it, this bridge of no return, I thought. Below is a dark canyon where water churns, and hungry bears roam. I will not fall. The bridge will hold. It's a lesson in trust.

I had no idea what to expect of grief, but I was not expecting the rage that burnt in me. It was white hot, a heat I had never known. It consumed most of my energy, and keeping it from my children took the rest. There is evidence in the F**Ks scrawled in huge letters across my notebook. The pages are torn where I pressed so hard, the edges singed with the heat of it.

When my mother died, it was like a building being torn down,

opening up a view to things that had previously been hidden.
What shocked me the most was that my anger was not so much
about the tearing down, as about what was revealed in the space
where she used to stand. It was immense. It felt like everything
carried by every maternal ancestor was being burnt up through
me. I think my mum knew it was coming. Before she went into
hospital she had said, in words uncharacteristic of the way she
spoke, 'Don't let the trauma of this live in your body and make
you ill. Make sure you get it out.'

I worked with my anger. I meditated. I went to the sea and
screamed into the waves. I ran. I wrote. I took the words of fire
and flame, threw them into a bowl, struck a match and set light
to all they contained. It burnt and I was burning too.

I was afraid of the flames spreading to other parts of my life,
so I decided to go away for a while, and signed up last minute for
a writing retreat at Cabilla[1] on Bodmin Moor. I had heard that
it was a special place of ancient woodland and rivers, temperate
rainforest and wildflower meadows, and one of my favourite poets
was teaching. Nobody told me magic was going to happen.

On the second morning, I got a text message which showed
me something I could never unsee. The anger that had begun
to subside raged in me once more. I snuck off to the far corner
of a field to call someone close to me, who assured me that my
response was valid. After a long conversation I felt a little calmer,
but there was still anger swirling in my body as I hung up and
went over to the clearing where morning yoga was taking place.

I apologised for being late, took the last available mat and
stretched out. As soon as I reached my right arm forward, a moth
flew down and landed on it. Little more than an inch long, she had
a long straight nose, and the line of silver along the edges of her
folded wings made it look like she was wearing a magical cloak.

I never harm insects and flying creatures, but my instinct is to brush them off. Not this time. I felt instantly soothed by this beautiful moth. She stayed on my arm for the entire yoga class. Leah, who was on the mat next to me, leant over and whispered that in Hawaii, where she lives, moths are thought to be the spirits of the departed in transition, bringing a spiritual message to a loved one. I later learnt that many people in Japan believe the same thing about winged creatures.

By the end of breakfast the moth, who was still on my arm, had become the talk of the retreat. I went for a long walk, did some writing and had lunch, and still she stayed with me.

I had never had such an experience. The moth made me feel comforted, while also feeling like she was asking for my protection. 'I've got you, Mum,' I found myself saying. It felt like she had me too, and that she had come to help ease my anger, which was dissipating with every passing hour.

That afternoon, I wanted to go for a swim in the river, so I laid some leaves on a poetry book in my cabin, put out a small dish of water, and asked the moth to stay there while I swam. She hopped off my arm and onto the floor. When I returned an hour later she was in the same spot. I put my arm down alongside her, and she hopped back on. It was not until later, when my *kokoro* felt settled – more than ten hours after she had first arrived on my yoga mat – that she flew away.

I remember being afraid that after my mother had gone I would feel like I was riding the wave of time into the future, away from her, but the moth made me recognise an unexpected and wholly welcome by-product of contemplating Dōgen's view of time. I was not being carried away from her at all. No, she was here with me inside every moment, along with everything else.

After the retreat, I posted a photo on social media asking for help in identifying the moth. It turned out to be a *Chrysoteuchia culmella*. Of course it was. My mother's name was Christine, known to all her friends as Chris.

Ashes and bone

I didn't tell anyone about the nightmares I had after the cremation, visions of her body burning. Her face was serene and there was no pain, but she was on fire. I saw flames dance across the purple veins in her thin hands, and the collar bone where the water had pooled in the bath the night before she died. Her arms, which had offered so many hugs. The legs that had walked miles with my children in pushchairs when they were small. The hair she loved to have styled, and her blue, blue eyes. All of it burning, turning to ash. It scorched my heart and filled my lungs with smoke.

Almost everyone in Japan is cremated these days. In a ceremony known as *kotsuage* (骨上げ), 'lifting of the bones', the family gathers after the cremation to remove any remaining bone fragments from the ash with long chopsticks. The first time I learnt of this custom, I shuddered. It was so far removed from the way that we deal with death in my own country, it was hard to imagine. Some people say it helps them cope with the reality of the loss. Thinking about my mum's ashes in the urn at her home, I found it hard to make the connection between those dusty remains and the person who gave birth to me.

In Dōgen's *Shōbōgenzō*, there is a famous passage about firewood and ashes which says, 'Firewood becomes ash, and does not become firewood again. Yet do not suppose that the ash is after and the firewood before.'[2]

I carried this passage around with me, searching for a way

to turn the ashes back to firewood, fighting the knowledge that it was impossible; that things are as they are in each and every moment.

With hindsight it seems to me that grief of any kind has the power to incinerate life as we know it, and it is up to those of us left behind to trawl through today's ashes to pick out the bones of what went before: the memories, the life lessons, the shared stories and the evidence of love. It is a morbid, heartbreaking job, but I have a feeling that it might be essential to our survival.

The words from the oracle card reading rose up again:

Ask the questions other people do not ask.

What if midlife, and other pivotal life transitions, such as marriage, divorce, graduations, empty-nesting, career changes and retirement, are a burning too? What if my job right now is to pick through the ashes of all that has gone before, and lift out the bones that remain? To choose the memories I will carry tucked into a pocket in my heart. To accept the lessons life has already taught me, while opening to those I have yet to learn. To acknowledge all I am grateful for, having lived those years so far. And to see that ash is ash. It cannot be firewood now, but the ash can nourish the roots of something new.

My one comfort during that time was the knowledge that nothing had gone unsaid. My mother knew how much we loved her, and we knew how much she loved us. I was so grateful that we had not put off the conversations we needed to have.

My mind drifted back to a chance encounter in a cemetery in the far west of Kyoto the previous year. I had wandered into the entrance of a small temple, curious about a statue sitting among the bushes.

'Hello,' a gentle voice called from over my right shoulder.

'Oh, hello. I just came in to look at this statue. I hope that's OK,' I said, turning round to see a kind-looking, elderly lady shuffling towards me.

'Oh, I don't work here. I've come to visit my mother's grave. She died twenty-six years ago today. Here, let me show you.'

Before I knew it, I was following the lady, who introduced herself as Mrs Matsumoto, into the cemetery next door, and being introduced to her family plot. I didn't really know what to say, so I asked Matsumoto-san about her mother. 'What kind of a woman was she?'

Just as she began to tell me, another lady came bustling into the cemetery, carrying a large bunch of leaves. 'Here's my sister,' Matsumoto-san said, introducing us to each other. 'We always meet here on the anniversary of Mother's death.' Turning to her sister, she said, 'This young lady was just asking me about Mother, and about her life when she was young.'

And so began an hour of reminiscing about their childhoods and recalling their mother's stories of how hard life had been after the war, when they were so poor they had to forage for grass to eat. They spoke of the men they had lost to battle, and of their mother's resilience, and all the fun they had when they were young despite the hardship. They were both laughing at one particular story when Matsumoto-san began to cry.

'Are you okay?' I asked.

'Since Mother died twenty-six years ago, we have never spoken like this, me and my sister,' she said.

Her sister looked down at the ground and shook her head.

'I can die happy now because we have had this conversation.

I think Mother sent you here today so we could have this talk. Why else would a foreigner appear in our cemetery on the anniversary of her death?'

It was this conversation that had made me vow to myself not to leave anything unsaid between me and my own mother, and I was glad of it.

Finding my way

The untethered feeling lingered for a long while. Unsure of what to do next, I did another oracle reading, asking for guidance on how to navigate this time.

The card I pulled was arresting. It told of an ego collapse, and that the only way through this time was to dissolve who I thought I was, to become who I am destined to be. As soon as I read it I knew the process had already begun.

My edges felt blurry, as if the layers I had so carefully built up over the years were flaking off and being carried away in the wind. And I didn't care, which was surprising.

The cards warned of emotional turmoil ahead, and a great alchemical reckoning afoot. Surely not. Surely the tough part was behind me.

Back in autumn, when I had been in Japan to climb Hagurosan in the season of blazing *momiji* leaves, and to interview Master Hoshino at his pilgrim lodge at the foot of the mountain, I had asked about *yamabushi* training. He said, 'You have to experience it to understand. Why don't you try it some time?'

Yamabushi training, which is open to anyone willing to travel to remote Japanese mountains to participate, had a reputation for being one of the toughest spiritual trainings in the world. I had heard many stories about it over the years, about fasting and fire jumping, meditating under freezing waterfalls and climbing mountains in the middle of the night. I had always been curious, but it was extreme, and I would soon be pushing fifty. So I smiled a non-committal smile, and moved on to my next question.

It had been my intention to climb Gassan back then, in a go-slow-and-take-lots-of-snack-breaks kind of way, but just before I set off on my trip last October, my phone had pinged with a Line App message. It was my friend Kōji, an ultramarathon runner and serious climber. His photos showed a whiteout on Gassan from his visit the previous day. 'It was so very cold,' he said. 'There is snow everywhere. I think it's too late.'

Even though I had taken the first plane I could after the borders opened post-pandemic, the mountain had closed for the winter. I was gutted. I had missed the hiking window by a matter of days. Come spring, there would be skiing on its lower slopes all the way through to July, but the mountain wouldn't fully open again until the summer, and that had seemed so far away.

When my mum died, the image of Gassan kept returning to me. I sent a message to one of the *yamabushi*, asking if I could arrange an accompanied hike some time. Many Japanese people believe Gassan is home to the spirits of their ancestors and I wondered if it would help, somehow, to be there. 'Of course,' he said, 'but before that, allow me to take your mother's name up the mountain, and pray for her spirit at the shrine at the top.' I was so moved I didn't know what to say.

The more I thought about the hike, the more I wondered whether I should just go the whole way and undergo *yamabushi* training.[3] I was terrified of the physical and mental challenge, and wary of the secret rituals, but I couldn't get the image of the mountain out of my head.

If my mother could face death with such courage, surely I could face Gassan.

KOKORO WORK: FALLING

- What endings are you grieving? What beginnings did or might they bring about?
- What is the most thoughtful or helpful thing someone has said or done to help you in your grief or loss?
- Is there anything unsaid between you and people you love? If they are no longer alive, write down what you want to say. If they are still alive, why not write them a letter, have a conversation or reach out another way?

KOKORO WISDOM

A life well lived is a life infused with the bittersweetness of love.

When we lose someone we love, it is the *kokoro* that does the work of alchemising our grief, and reminds us that the greater the pain, the more we loved and were loved.

CHAPTER 7

RELEASE

Travelling light

Scrambling up a wall of boulders using muscles I did not know I had, I felt nauseous, ached everywhere, and was in equal parts fascinated and repelled by the sweat pouring off the back of my hands. We had risen in the dark and begun climbing hours ago, while the moon was still high.

I had two plain *onigiri* rice balls in my backpack but had no idea when I would get to eat them. I hadn't eaten anything since the day before. I was not used to fasting, and struggled with not knowing when the next meal would come.

Normally, I research things, but for *yamabushi* training I had purposely avoided trying to find out too much. We were advised not to ask too many questions in advance because 'information gets in the way'. One of the things I had read, though, was that the training integrates the Buddhist idea of the ten realms of existence: the six mundane realms (hell-dwellers, hungry ghosts, beasts, demigods, humans, heavenly beings) and the four higher realms that characterise the path to Buddhahood.[1] As we went deeper into our training, it felt like we were navigating all ten realms at once.

I stank. I had never felt so filthy. No washing or teeth brushing was allowed. We wore the same clothes day after day, putting them on in the dark each morning when they were still wet with the previous day's sweat. This was the realm of the beasts, I guessed. I couldn't ask because we weren't allowed to speak. Other than chanted prayers, the only word we were permitted to utter was *uketamō,* familiar from my autumn hike up Hagurosan as 'I accept (everything and anything)'.

When we weren't climbing we were often sitting in the traditional Japanese posture known as *seiza*, feet slowly going numb beneath us as we meditated. It was the peak of summer, but the *shukubō* pilgrim lodge had no air conditioning, so we sat and we sweated.

At night, I lay awake for hours on the hard floor in a room filled with snoring bodies, trying to ignore the insects feasting on my tired body and wondering what in hell I was doing there. As soon as I finally drifted off I was rudely awakened by the penetrating sound of the *horagai* conch, just a few feet away.

The overhead lights came on and we had to put our thin futons away and use the outdoor toilet in the dark before the second *horagai* sounded. That was the signal to get dressed in our complicated *shiroshozoku* outfits, still stiff with yesterday's sweat, before the third *horagai* sounded, by which point we had to be outside, lined up in the dark with our white *jika tabi* (split-toed boots) done up, carrying a wooden staff, ready to go.

As I stood there under the moon, feeling woozy and disorientated, I remembered that as much as I had wanted to come I had also been dreading this day. Our training required us to climb three mountains in three days, and that day it was the turn of Gassan.

Many people believe that the souls of departed humans undergo forty-nine days of training on lower slopes elsewhere and then travel to Gassan – the mountain we were just about to climb in the dark – where they are deified and remain for eternity, taking care of the living. According to this belief, the spirits of infinite past generations were within whispering distance.

There were twenty-four of us in all, fourteen Japanese women, nine Japanese men and me, in varying states of readiness. Due to the rule of silence, I knew nothing of the people I was climbing with, not even their names. This was highly unusual in Japan, where introductions are paramount and usually begin with a company or group affiliation followed by the name, offered in the possessive, such as '*Hitachi no Tanaka desu*', 'I am Tanaka from Hitachi', where *no* means 'belonging to'. Instead, there on the mountain it was the opposite:

We were nameless, belonging to nowhere and no one but ourselves and to nature itself.

Given all that had happened in recent months, Gassan was the mountain I was most intrigued by and most nervous to climb.

The heat was blistering, and the pace brutal. Gassan rose almost two kilometres into the sky. Any sensible person would have trained for it. My preparation had consisted of four months of grief, a six-thousand-mile journey with two small children, a holiday gone wrong and a pulled shoulder muscle from handling my rucksack awkwardly as I left for the mountains.

Far from a holiday

Rather than my travelling to Japan alone again to undertake the training, Mr K and I had decided to take the girls there for the summer and to rent a little *machiya* house in Kyoto. It sounded dreamy, but when I look back now I can see that we didn't really think it through.

We landed. We melted. We celebrated an eighth birthday

at Disneyland on the hottest day of the year. We went to more convenience stores in three days than I had been to in my life.

I tried to focus on the basics: stay cool and hydrated, find food they will eat, be spontaneous, have fun. It was easier said than done when I didn't recognise myself. I am normally a calm, curious and flexible traveller, especially in Japan. I had hoped to leave the stress of the past few months behind, but it turned out I had brought it with me, and I was on edge, impatient and shattered. There was a flood of difficult news from back home, too – an impending divorce, a house sale fallen through, a broken engagement. Everything was melting in the heat.

After a couple of days of Tokyo overwhelm – noise, lights, humidity, tall buildings not suitable for small children who don't like lifts, and so on – we took the bullet train to Kyoto. Mr K and I relaxed into our seats and watched for Mount Fuji out of the right-hand window, excited to be heading to a city we both loved, and to share our memories with our children.

It turned out they were completely uninterested in any stories of Kyoto before their time. They were only interested in the Kyoto that was in front of their faces – the squishy toys and the manga posters and the line-up of cute animal-shaped donuts. For a while I was frustrated that they were not open to all the things I wanted to show them, but then one day their excitement about the wild monkey park pierced my shell and I realised that their version mattered too.

Japan is a feeling. I had been running round the city, trying to show the children my favourite places, offer them food that I thought was delicious and introduce them to people who made me feel at home. But a feeling is not something we can teach someone else; it is something that bubbles up from somewhere deep within. It is our response to the world from within the *kokoro*. And we each have to discover that for ourselves.

I knew that the image of delight on their faces as they fed fish-flavoured ice lollies to fluffy kittens at the cat cafe would soon only exist as another smoky layer of memory, so I bent down and stroked the cats, and purred gently alongside them.

Ten days into our trip, there was an Instagram version filled with smiles and gorgeous places, which was real, and there was another version of meltdowns and more, which was also real. Naively perhaps, I had not anticipated that a long trip overseas with children would be so exhausting. And yet in the middle of it all, there was a huge prayer of gratitude that we got to be together, making memories in such a special place. It was confusing, and challenging, and not relaxing at all.

One evening, after a particularly difficult bedtime which ended with one of the girls shouting, 'I want to go home', Mr K suggested that he take the girls back early, and leave me in Japan on my own for several more weeks, to do what I needed to do; by which he meant writing, but also everything else that he could sense was unfinished.

I said no at first, and then I said, actually yes, and then I cried, feeling like a huge failure. I have experienced Kyoto summers before. What did I expect? The children had lost their beloved grandma, and were tired at the end of a long school year. What did I expect? I was trying to have a holiday at the same time as grieving my mother and writing a book. What did I expect? Travelling anywhere with children takes all your reserves. We had no reserves. What did I expect?

We booked new flights home for Mr K and the girls, tried not to think about the wasted money and focused on togethering for the remainder of their trip. Somehow, the knowledge that it would be over soon changed everything, and it was a special time for us all.

Some nights, we went for early evening walks when the air was cooler. In many Japanese ghost tales there is a particular time of day known as *ōmagatoki* (逢魔時) around twilight, when strange things step out of the shadows and the imaginal comes to life. The night before they left, walking the streets of Kyoto at that hour, their small hands in mine, I felt a pull to turn around. I swear I saw a trail of silvery grey dust behind me, like tiny flakes of ash drifting in the moonlight.

Remainder

My family left on a midnight plane to Dubai and sleep taunted me like a ghost, hovering yet not quite arriving. I tried not to think of how everything most precious to me was hurtling around the planet in a metal tube. I berated myself for not having planned better. For not having been more patient. I was sick with something that felt like the flu. I got up while it was still dark and looked in the bathroom mirror. My face was lopsided and puffy with dark triangles under my eyes. Despite the joy-filled last few days, I still felt like a failure. I could see every drop of grief laid out in the deep creases of my face. I had a suntan but somehow looked grey. My hair was flat. I didn't recognise myself – again.

I lit a candle, made some tea, and listened for traces of my family's laughter soaked into the walls. There is a beautiful term in Japanese, *hikikomogomo* (悲喜交々), which means having alternating feelings of joy and sorrow in your heart, tasting the bittersweetness of life. I had felt this often over the past few months, and it lingered in our little rented *machiya* once my family had gone. Loss and love, frustration and laughter, shadow and light, numbness and aliveness, shattering and gratitude.

Their leaving coincided with my plan to travel north for *yamabushi* training. I took a bullet train to Tokyo, and another onward to Shinjō.

An hour out from Tokyo and there were paddy fields, small towns and villages, and some wilder areas of green. In Fukushima, it was raining. Parasols swapped out for umbrellas, footsteps sped up. Soon there was a gorge, low forested mountains and no houses for a while. Further north still, the remote region of Dewa Sanzan was waiting.

I caught my reflection in the bullet train window as we shot into a tunnel. I looked old. Boring, dressed in beige, hair scraped back into a bun to keep cool in the heat. A stereotype of middle-aged. But my lucky feather necklace glinted back at me from the train window and promised adventure.

Mountain of myth

And so I came to find myself standing half-dressed, half-asleep in the dark, preparing to face Gassan. The sacred peak, which means 'Moon Mountain', takes its name from Tsukuyomi-no-Mikoto, the god of the moon and ruler of the night. Tsukuyomi is enshrined on Gassan, so it felt somehow appropriate, if deeply uncomfortable, for us to begin our ascent while the moon was still high.

You might remember I mentioned that this mountain, which is covered in snow for most of the year, is known as a gathering place for ancestral spirits. I don't know what happens when we die. No one does. I don't know if a spirit separates from our body and climbs a mountain. I don't know if we are simply gone and our bodies return to the earth as organic matter. I don't know if there is such a thing as karma, or reincarnation, or heaven. In Japan, you will find people who believe in all of these things, and people who believe in none of them. One thing I did know was that Gassan, known as the mountain of death, was like no place I had ever been before.

Our guide was Master Hoshino himself, one of the few living *yamabushi* to have undergone the intensive one-hundred-day *fuyu-no-mineiri* winter peak training on Dewa Sanzan. He was dressed in a spotless white outfit, with a bell tied at his waist and a conch in his hand. With a long white beard and a twinkle in his eye, he could have been a sage from any century.

Master Hoshino led us through the wide fields on the lower slopes of Gassan. It was a fairly gentle beginning. I was acutely aware that Mr K and the girls were on a flight from Dubai to London. Phones were banned during training, so I had no way of reaching them. I thought being high on a mountain might make me feel closer to them somehow. Instead, it just made me feel sick.

Once the path turned to rocks, I had to concentrate on the feet of the person in front of me, using a wooden staff for balance, at times scrambling over rocks two feet high. My body was doing the thinking, and my mind cleared.

As the sun came up it revealed the distant peak of Chōkai-san and a series of low mountains in the distance arranged like a collage of tissue-paper blues. Every time I looked up the view was different – a small lake, a meadow filled with flowers, an *unkai* – a sea of clouds.

There can be a vastness to landscape
which echoes the scale of the
kokoro's capacity for feeling.

I felt all of it up on Gassan. Every now and then, we would pause to pray at a sacred place. Bells, claps, chanting, the haunting call of the *horagai*. This repeated ritual had a profound effect on me. Each vibration rippled through my heart space. Something was opening.

I carried a deep sense of loss but also a growing sense of spaciousness. I had been wandering the landscape of my heart without a map, unsure of what I was seeking. Something was finally emerging, although I had no name for it.

Climbing the upper slopes of Gassan was not easy. At one point I hit a wall of exhaustion and thought I could not go on, but at that precise moment a breeze blew in from nowhere, pouring strength into my quadriceps, and I found myself powering on with unexpected ease. It was the strangest thing. From then on, I noticed that although my head often told me my body was flagging, when I actually dropped into that body, I felt strong.

Reaching to the sky

It was a scorching hot day, and Gassan was bathed in sunlight for most of the climb, until one particular point near the top, where patches of snow appeared and the sky turned grey. As it darkened, it felt like we were entering some kind of void, a fertile darkness, the domain of ghosts. The heart of the mountain beat with the rhythm of the ancients and I shivered, despite the lingering heat.

At the top of Gassan there is a shrine, and, just behind it, there is an area that is cordoned off by an inconspicuous rope. I didn't even notice it until Master Hoshino indicated that we should leave the path at that point and climb higher, to the true summit of the mountain. I would learn later that this is a holy space sealed off for sacred rites. It was where the *yamabushi* would be lighting the annual bonfire a few days from now, to send the resident spirits off the mountain, back to their hometowns all across Japan, to be reunited with their descendants for the Obon festival.

At the top, we lined up in silence behind Master Hoshino, bowing our heads. He rang his bell, blew long plaintive notes on the *horagai*, sang an invocation, and we began to chant *Hannya Shingyō*, the Heart Sutra, once more.

The domain of the spirits is a liminal space – another dimension of time where everyday rules do not apply. A wall of mist rose up around us, and I realised I could still see the moon, silvery and high. From somewhere in the silence I heard the words 'prayer is surrender', and then I realised I was crying. Standing on the summit of Gassan, the mountain of death, I could no longer see the mountain at all. Through my tears, I could only see the mist and the daytime moon and a glimpse of the invisible.

In his luminous book *Each Moment is the Universe*, Dainin Katagiri called the present moment 'the pivot of nothingness', saying:

At that precise point – the intersection of time and space, which is called right now, right here – all sentient beings come together into the moment and a vast world comes up: past, present, future, earth, trees, planets, moons, and suns.[2]

This was palpable at the summit of Gassan, and out of the mist arrived the strangest, clearest, most profound realisation:

I am not afraid to die.

It echoed the words my mother had spoken to me in her final days, but it made no logical sense.

I absolutely do not want to die yet. For a long time, in fact, as long as I am healthy and my loved ones need me, I want to be amazed by this beautiful world over and over again. I want to be an active part of my children's lives for as long as possible. I want to grow old with my husband. I have many more poems to read and books to write, conversations to have, places to explore and whole worlds inside myself to discover. My work is far from done. So what did it mean?

Master Hoshino blew his conch once more and the words came again. *I am not afraid to die.* This was not a message from my rational mind. It came straight from my *kokoro*.

I looked up to the sky and everything else fell away. I could see right into the eye of the moment, the vast, expansive potential right there, right then, on the mountain, in this world, in my life, in all of our lives. I could be whoever I wanted to be. Not being afraid to die meant not being afraid to let go of any and all notions of who I thought I was. It did not mean I had to start over, but it meant I *could*, at any time. It was an invitation to let go of any fixed idea of who I had to be.

I could cast aside any labels I had taken on or that had been put upon me, and be free to reinvent myself at any moment. And I was no longer afraid to die over and over again in this life in order to see each moment anew.

I was not afraid to let other things die too – the stories I carried about how I had to show up in the world. The friendships that no longer nourished. The projects that had once felt so right but which no longer felt aligned. The inherited framework by which I had been measuring success for as long as I could remember. The ideas I had about how things should be in any particular phase of life. I was not afraid to let it all die. And in amongst it all I sensed the death of my anger, which I buried on the mountain that day.

What matters is that we live with love, from the *kokoro*, responding to the beauty and the sorrow, the darkness and the light of the world in each moment, as it arises. We must remember that life itself is a kind of prayer, and every day is sacred.

Descent

We descended the mountain so fast I thought I might break an ankle, but my wooden staff became an extension of my limbs, and I felt like a mountain goat – strong, blessed, joyful. My *jika tabi* left a trail of sparks as I flew down the slopes.

> It turns out I was stronger than
> I knew. We all are.

When the training was over and it was time to head back to Kyoto, I took a moment to sit in the garden of the pilgrim lodge and breathe. I sensed movement, and my eyes were drawn to one particular tree, where a haiku was waiting.

> *sky drifts to nothing*
> *twitching on the lowest branch*
> *sparrow knows it's time*

I could not wait any longer. There was something I had to do.

KOKORO WORK: RELEASE

- Where in your own life do you sense *hikikomogomo* – the bittersweetness of joy and sorrow alternating in your heart?
- What would be different if you were not afraid to die?
- What have you been putting off that it is now time to do?

🜔

KOKORO WISDOM

A life well lived is a series of mountains climbed.

Our rational mind has a tendency to try to protect us by encouraging us to quit when things get tough, but when we can drop into the body, tune in to the wisdom of the *kokoro* and tune out the doubts, we are capable of so much more than we know.

CHAPTER 8

AGEING

Layers of life

The taxi delivered me to Hirosawa Pond, a serene place often missed by the tourists, who throng to the famous bamboo forest at nearby Arashiyama. As a teenager I lived with a Japanese family down the road, and every day I would return from school, slide open the front door calling, '*Tadaima*' ('I'm home'), and check the bottom step of the wooden stairs. If there were any letters waiting for me, without removing my shoes I would lean over and grab them, pop them in my backpack and head straight back out with an '*Itte kimasu*' – 'See you later!'[1]

I always took my letters to the lake. Back in those days, university friends sent news by snail mail, often on thin, blue aerogramme paper, each person's handwriting promising college gossip and inducing a flicker of homesickness. Many of the letters – at least one a week – were from my mum, carrying news from home. They always made me feel directly connected across space and time, despite the time difference and the six thousand miles between us.

Before she died, my mum wrote me a final letter. As soon as my older brother handed it to me, I knew I wanted to open it there, at Hirosawa Pond. I couldn't bear to open it before then anyway. When we first arrived in Kyoto, I had held it up to my face, searching for the scent of her perfume, and then squirrelled it away in my suitcase, still not ready, knowing that once it was done, there would be nothing else waiting. But now, three months on from her death, I finally felt as ready as I would ever be.

I had carefully placed the letter in the inside pocket of my handbag, and put on a new green dress. I had been so sure I would be devastated all over again I hadn't bothered with any makeup, but it didn't turn out like that at all.

As I stepped out of the taxi I was greeted by the sound of children's laughter spilling all over the tiny island shrine, which reached out into the lake. It was a gorgeous sunny day and my dress matched the colour of the water exactly. Kites swooped overhead and the children – a similar age to my own – were fishing with handmade rods cobbled together from disposable wooden chopsticks and string, using squid guts as bait. A huge black crow perched on a post at the edge of a nearby rice field, watching, and iridescent blue dragonflies zipped around. The children issued delighted squeals every time they caught another *zarigani*, a kind of small crayfish. It felt as if my mum had sent them to remind me of the simple joys in life, the wonder of childhood, and how the cycle of life continues.

Surrounded by their joy, I sat beneath an old pine at the water's edge and opened the letter, which began 'I could write endless pages about why I love you . . .' It was a simple, precious two pages, written in my older brother's hand when my mother was too weak to hold a pen, other than to write my name at the top and sign off 'Love Mum' at the end.

'I am so proud of you,' she wrote, 'but you don't need to make me or anyone else proud. The most important thing is that you are happy.'

I was not expecting that.

With this final breath, my mother blew away the version of success I had held on to so tightly all my life. *You do not need to make anyone else proud. The most important thing is that you are happy.*

This was coming from a woman who had spent decades reminding us of the importance of education, celebrating our achievements and encouraging us to go after our dreams. A woman who thought that respectability was next to godliness and that a university degree gave you bonus points as a human being (she didn't have one). Perhaps this was one of the many things she had got clarity on in her final days, once she had left that coat of regret and worry at the consultant's office.

With this, my mother confirmed something I had long felt was true for me, but had resisted with my logical mind:

> Success has nothing to do with your outer life and what other people think of you. It's about the richness of your inner life, and the way you show up in the world with genuine consideration for others.
>
> And it's about the joy, beauty and wonder that you find in the world, and how you share that through the way that you live.

By these measures, my mother had lived a beautiful life. The irony of needing her permission before I fully believed this new story of success was not lost on me. How about you, I wonder? How do or will you measure your own life?

I looked up at the lake I had been visiting for nearly thirty years and for the first time ever, I saw a turtle swimming by. A symbol of support and good luck, apparently. A talisman for the road ahead.

*

Each August, at dusk on the night of the Gozan no Okuribi ritual fires of Obon, hundreds of floating lanterns are sent drifting across Hirosawa Pond, sending ancestral spirits on their way. It has been a famous moon-viewing site since the Heian period. One samurai lord of that time, Minamoto no Yorimasa, wrote a famous *waka* poem about the lake in which he contemplated whether, in ancient times, folk had left their shadows by the water's edge.[2] Sitting there, nine hundred years later, I knew exactly what he meant.

The day I opened my mum's last letter at Hirosawa Pond, I sensed the shadows of my own younger selves lined up at the water's edge. I felt like I could reach out and pierce time with a needle, stitching together all the versions of myself that had visited the lake before – in my teens, twenties, thirties and forties – like tracing paper cut-outs held together with thread. And it was not the first time I had encountered my younger self in recent months.

Meeting each other, meeting ourselves

When I first heard about the university reunion I had thought little about it. Reunions have a reputation for being dreadful occasions where people brag, cringe or embarrass themselves and I had no desire to do any of those things. But then I heard that a dear friend was organising a table for dinner, and some of my favourite people from long ago were attending, so I signed up. We had a wonderful weekend in the cathedral city of Durham, where we had studied together many years before. We laughed, cried and danced until four in the morning. One of my friends, a headteacher and mother of two boys, stood at the bar as morning neared and cried, 'I don't want this night to end.'

To delay the inevitable, and for old times' sake, everyone came back to the hotel room I was sharing with a friend. Instead of the vodka of old, we had tea and ginger biscuits to soak up some of the night's alcohol, knowing that hangovers hit us harder these days. There was more laughing, sharing of memories, talk of the trials of midlife and a joy in remembering that the gathered people knew us in a way many others never would, having known us back when we were more porous, before society had the chance to tell us what was what, before we were conditioned into thinking that labels really mattered and the only way was up. That weekend reminded me that our people care about us more than we allow ourselves to believe, and care about what we do a lot less than we convince ourselves is true.

Many of the themes that came up in conversations at the reunion had come up again and again over the past few years with local friends, in my online community, as well as with my contemporaries in Japan. The contexts might be different, but the challenges seemed virtually universal:

> ## To navigate any major life transition, including midlife, is to navigate grief.

There might be grief for our changing relationships with ageing parents and our growing children, or for the children we couldn't have, for the people and pets we have lost and the days we cannot share with them, for friendships that didn't make it, for relationships that have fallen apart, for the paths we did not choose and the decisions we regret, the people we lost touch with, the ways we did not celebrate, the things we missed in our desperate rush to be successful. And there is anticipatory grief as we stand at any major life threshold, for the things we now know we have to let die in order for us to fully live, for the people we know we will lose along the way and for the paths we cannot choose – because we cannot walk them all in this limited allocation of time and space that we call life.

Often, this grief is left unnamed and untended, so it wreaks havoc in our lives. We must acknowledge it all, get support where we need it, take good care of ourselves, and take the time to honour the person we have been at each stage, doing the best they could with the information they had and the situation they were in.

In the Japanese language, the most common word for regret is *kōkai* (後悔), which literally translates as 'after-poison'. We suffer enough already. Let's not poison ourselves too. We are vital and alive and each moment is a new opportunity to make the most of what we do still have available to us – an expansive, beautiful world full of many good people and much poetry, beauty and magic.

On the Monday after the weekend before, when most of my friends had left Durham to return to their lives in various cities around the world, I walked up the hill past my old college and into the university's ten-hectare Botanic Garden, which had been one of my favourite places to practise the ritual dialogues in my Japanese textbook, with only the trees listening. I thought the visit might bring back some memories, but I wasn't expecting a face-to-face encounter with my twenty-two-year-old self.

She was already there when I arrived, at the stone semicircle on the far side of the Japanese garden, rehearsing for her final exams. If she passed them, there was a job waiting for her in Japan. She was pretending to be in a business meeting, negotiating something or other. Then she made a mistake and pulled a folded piece of paper out of her pocket, checked it and started again. I could tell she was frustrated with herself for getting it wrong, and wanted to give her a hug.

You'll get there, I whispered.

She turned her head to look in my direction, as if she had heard something, and then carried on.

As the ghost of my twenty-two-year-old self practised for an exam I knew she'd pass, I told her what the next couple of decades would bring. How she would keep learning, and the more she learnt the more she would realise all she did not know, and that one day she would be okay with that. How she would travel the world, spend many years in Japan, make mistakes over and over again, write poetry, write books, write too many sympathy cards, and not enough love letters.

I looked beyond her at the silhouettes of trees, to the outline of a building I didn't remember, and told her things I wanted her to know: that those she counted as her friends were precious, and that she would make more; that the boys who would leave her needed to do that so she could meet Mr K and have two beautiful daughters (although that wouldn't happen for a long time); that one day she would quit the corporate world to do what she loved; and sometimes doing what she loved would be the easiest thing in the world, and sometimes it would be hard, but it would always be worth it.

I thanked her for choosing Japanese, and told her that it would weave its way through her life in ways she couldn't even imagine. I told her to be open to friendships with people of all ages, and to remember that we never really know what is going on for others, so to be kind, always.

I told her that the world would change so much, so fast in the coming years, but she just needed to stay curious to avoid getting overwhelmed by it all.

She pushed her dyed blonde hair back behind her ears, checked her notes again, stuffed them back in the pocket of her purple jeans, and launched into the next piece.

I kept talking, no longer sure where the words were coming from: 'Anytime you feel lost, look up to the night sky, and let the moon and the stars remind you that life is a miracle, and in the grand scheme of things, most of the things that you will worry about do not matter at all. Don't cling to stuff or people or ideas. Take risks. Good unknowns usually lie on the other side, and you'll learn something along the way. Stop worrying so much about what other people think. It just gets in the way. If you try to think your way through life, you will be restricted to choices within the limits of what you intellectually know. But if you feel your way through it, and respond to the world from your *kokoro*, you will have the full expanse of possibility open to you, and you will always know, deep down, what to do.'

She had stopped rehearsing by then and was staring out at the trees, as if listening. I leant towards her and whispered:

Live your life and love your people.
Nothing lasts for ever.

When the words left my mouth, they sounded like a remembering.

I remembered them again as I walked away from Hirosawa Pond, looking around slowly, taking it all in, and wondering when I would next return, if ever, and if I did, whether today's version of me would be waiting as a shadow by the water's edge.

The festival of ten thousand lanterns

Perhaps it was no coincidence that all these thoughts about life and death had been swirling in August, as Japan celebrated its annual Obon festival, when ancestral spirits are said to return to their homes to feast and converse with the living. On the final day of the holiday, I felt drawn to go to the Mantōe Festival of Ten Thousand Lanterns at Higashi Ōtani cemetery. I had never been to a festival in a graveyard before – it would have felt like an intrusion and, to be honest, it seemed morbid. But this year I felt invited.

The path up to the cemetery was strung with lanterns, as was every staircase and every platform of graves cut into the hillside. Each one held a single candle, and many were decorated with children's drawings. I followed one family towards the top of the cemetery. They carried buckets for washing the graves, and bunches of *maki*, the yew plum pine branches that would be placed in the round containers attached to their plot. The families of the deceased laughed and joked as they went about their work, becoming serious only when it was time to pray, but even then there was a lightness to them. There was genial conversation and a sense of normality, as if they were popping in for tea.

I looked around at the orderly graves, vertical cuboids of grey stone standing to attention, as if on guard to protect the city and all who live in it. Most of the graves had been visited over the Obon holiday, and were freshly cleaned and decorated.

The beauty of the place was unexpected and suddenly overwhelming, and the dam burst. On the mountainside, looking out over the city I have loved for more than half my life, beneath the expanse of a clear evening sky, surrounded by ten thousand lanterns and the ashes of old bones, I finally fell apart in peace.

I could now see that the shredding had begun long before my mother's diagnosis. It had begun years ago, with the meltdown that led to me writing my first book *Freedom Seeker* aged thirty-nine, and it had continued through a search for home, the building of a business, the raising of a family, the unravelling of a friendship, the writing of several more books, my mother's death and the aftermath. The exhaustion of travelling to Japan in the blistering heat with two young children, followed by the intensity of the *yamabushi* training on Gassan, had simply been the mouse that sank the boat. My shredding finished with a flourish there and then in a strangely beautiful graveyard on the eastern edge of Kyoto.

My vision was blurred by the tears, but I wiped my eyes just in time to see the huge golden orb of the sun settle behind the mountains in the west. The sky was still a deep blue, carrying the remains of the day on the wings of wide clouds lit from below by the flare. This phenomenon, when the sun disappears but its light still illuminates the sky at twilight, is known as *ekō henshō* (回光返照), a term also used to describe the moment right before someone dies, when their life force is fully expressed and they glow.

Ekō henshō is also a familiar term in Zen. Dōgen used it in his instructions for meditation, where it is often translated as turning the light inward and illuminating the self, although more literally it means 'turning the light and returning the illumination'.[3] It reminded me of Yokoyama-san's description of the *kokoro* as a mechanism for taking in light and sending it back out to the world.

Ekō henshō is a threshold term, capturing a fleeting moment of change, which seemed to capture the in-betweenness I felt there in the cemetery. In that moment of illumination, after being willing to let so many things die, I realised that I had no idea what would take their place. Having let go of the measures of success I had carried all my life, how would I measure my life now? I sensed I might need to turn the light inwards for a while before I could send light back out into the world.

I recalled a passage I had read a couple of years back in a research paper called 'The Genealogy of Sorrow' by Akira Ōmine. It was about the Japanese view of life and death, and it had not made any sense to me at the time, but now I understood it completely:

> The bottom falls out of sorrow, so to speak, and one awakens to the depth of sorrow itself in which the small-minded, ego-centered sorrow is embraced. It is a dimension of sorrow which transcends sorrow without negating it; a sorrow that is no longer sorrow in the conventional sense, but also affirms it. No matter how deep the tragedy of life, there is an even deeper structure in life that embraces it and never abandons it to render it meaningless.[4]

The reason I understood it now was that when the bottom had fallen out of my life and I had awakened to the depth of life itself, in which the small-minded, ego-centred self was embraced, I could see that the vastness of life also embraced all old versions of myself without negating them. I had a feeling that this expansion of perspective might be the underlying structure of death and rebirth. Only time would tell.

I looked out across the city and beyond, to the mountains in the west. At that moment a distant cloud cracked open and a rainbow spilt out. I saw then that my quest had become a kind of *shōshin ryokō* (傷心旅行), a 'griefmoon', a sentimental journey undertaken as a balm for a wounded *kokoro*. They say time heals, but if Dōgen was right and time and existence are the same thing, perhaps it is living that heals.

Perhaps living fully is the most important job of all.

I stayed at Higashi Ōtani until darkness fell. The cemetery was alive with the flickering of ten thousand lanterns. It was the night of Gozan no Okuribi, when ritual bonfires are lit on the mountains around Kyoto to bid farewell to the visiting ancestral spirits. I imagined them rising up like smoke from every home across the city and all over Japan, gathering in the night sky and swirling their way back to Gassan.

I, too, had a mountain to get back to – Yudonosan, the mountain of rebirth and the future. If the births of my own children were anything to go by, it would be painful and messy, and there would be a lot more swearing before new life arrived.

KOKORO WORK: AGEING

- Divide your current age in half and imagine encountering yourself at that age. What would you say?
- What will you miss about this particular life stage when you move on to the next one?
- What has this reflection on death taught you about how you want to live?

心

KOKORO WISDOM

A life well lived is a life of integrated layers.

The *kokoro* changes and grows with us
as we age. There is valuable wisdom
available at every life stage.

湯殿山

PART THREE: YUDONOSAN

Rebirth on Sacred Spring Mountain

Whatever you carry, bring it here and set it down. Remove your shoes, stand before the priest and prepare yourself for the sacred ritual that awaits. All are welcome. Come, but speak not of what you find here, for the secrets of this mountain are for pilgrims alone to discover for themselves.

Every day is a chance for a new beginning on Yudonosan, Sacred Spring Mountain.

As the most mysterious of the three sacred mountains of Dewa Sanzan, Yudonosan is said to represent rebirth and the future. Yudono Shrine is known for its *goshintai* (御神体), a sacred object believed to be directly connected to a god. I will not tell you what it looks like, for visitors are forbidden to speak of what they find there. Perhaps one day you will go and see it for yourself.

The final part of our journey is inspired by this special place, offering an invitation to be intentional about how we want to live the rest of our lives, however long we may have left.

CHAPTER 9

RETURNING

Becoming who we are

To be honest, much of that day is a blur. It comes back in fragments. I know there was a huge red torii gate reaching to the clouds, and that as we filed silently beneath it, a large black bird swept across the sky. I remember being led along a series of secret paths, and I remember clambering down an earthen bank. I remember that we were split into two groups, men and women separately. When it was our turn, I took my cue from one of the veteran women to remove my *jika tabi* boots and *hakama* trousers, and hang them over a fallen tree trunk before scrambling down to the river barefoot. Then I was in icy water, and it was bliss to escape the heat but hard work to navigate slippery boulders while pushing upstream.

The next thing I remember is arriving at a huge hidden waterfall and being shocked by the enormity of its sound, which seemed to fill the sky. So this was *takigyō* (滝行), waterfall training.

The first time I went under I couldn't breathe, let alone meditate. It felt like the water was pummelling my insides directly, as if I was just a pair of lungs hovering in the vertical flow of water, being crushed like an aluminium can under the weight of it. I lasted less than ten seconds before the waterfall spat me out sideways onto a wall of rock. Shocked and embarrassed, I stumbled ungracefully across the uneven riverbed to the end of the queue and waited, trying to calm my breathing. I was going back under.

We were supposed to chant the Heart Sutra as we stood beneath the waterfall, but I didn't know the words well enough without my paper prompt, so instead I recited the lyrics of a song I co-wrote called 'The River', which was played at my mother's funeral: *There's a river* [gasp] *running through you* [gasp] / *and it'll flow* [gasp] *till the end of time.* / [gasp] *You've gotta trust in* [gasp] / *The way it's going,* [gasp] / *Let the river* [gasp] *lead you home.*

It wasn't easy to breathe, speak and stand upright, all at once. Somehow I managed to stay under for as long as it took to recite the whole song. By the end, my breathing was ragged, my body shivering, and my shoulders, neck and head numb from the pummelling, but I had done it.

I exited the flow and prostrated myself up against the wall of rock like a wild woman. I turned my face to one side and pressed it onto the rock for stability and comfort while I tried to get my breath back.

My first thought was, 'How the hell did I get here?' My second was, 'Why is there hot water running down my cheek?'

It took me a moment to realise that we must be directly beneath Yudono Shrine, considered to be the *okunoin* (the inner sanctum) of Dewa Sanzan. I hadn't expected to encounter the mountain of rebirth and the future quite like this.

The waterfall roared. Cold water rushed around my bare legs. Hot holy water streamed down my face. I felt battered by the flow and disorientated by the noise. I couldn't hear anything and yet somehow I could hear everything.

Waking up

As the water poured over me I had a strange sensation of seeing two realities at once: the reality of the waterfall, a natural phenomenon in a certain location – in this case an important *takigyō* spot for generations of *yamabushi* and their trainees. And then the reality of the individual droplets of water rushing in their millions over the rock face, and coming together in a given moment to make 'the waterfall', but then just a few instants later, having plunged into the river below and been sent downstream, no longer part of the phenomenon we call 'the waterfall'.

So what is it, exactly, which makes the waterfall 'the waterfall', I wondered, and where does it begin and end? If the individual elements of it are constantly changing, and it is never made up of exactly the same constituent elements in any two moments, is it only the label which holds it together? Or perhaps the label comes later, and before that it is simply a happening?

My mind wandered on. If a waterfall can be such a creature, as can other natural processes, what about human beings? We have labels, whether that be a name we are given or choose, or a job title, or simply 'human', but might we also be changing at the minutest level all the time? What if the label came later and before the label we were also just a happening? And where, exactly, do we humans begin and end?

Of course, like any idea that suddenly wakes us up, we look into it and realise many people have had that thought before; we just hadn't come across it. Later, I would further explore the work of theoretical physicist Carlo Rovelli and discover that he had explained something very similar from a scientific perspective:

Even the things that are most 'thing-like' are nothing more than long events. The hardest stone, in the light of what we have learnt from chemistry, from physics, from mineralogy, from geology, from psychology, is in reality a complex vibration of quantum fields, a momentary interaction of forces, a process that for a brief moment manages to keep its shape, to hold itself in equilibrium before disintegrating again into dust.[1]

We are time. We are happenings. We are fleeting sounds in the grand opera of the universe. Our lives are not only a collection of occurrences, where we collide with others in space and time; we too are events. Yet again we are reminded of *mujyō*, impermanence.

Perhaps, just like the waterfall, we are an ever-changing composite of the elements that shape us. We are remade over and over throughout our lives. We can let that process simply happen without our intervention, or we can proactively participate in the restoration, rejuvenation and recreation of our physical bodies and of our *kokoro* at any and every point in our lives.

To me, this is such an incredible thing to wake up to that it renders every one of my day-to-day worries ridiculous. It shouldn't take meditating under a waterfall on a remote Japanese mountain to realise this, but in my case it had.

We get stuck in these ideas about who we think we are and should be, we get shaped by the societies we live in and the opinions of others, and slowly, over time and as we age, these forms become fixed in our minds. But that is simply a construct of the imagination.

**Nothing is fixed. Everything is changing.
All possibilities are waiting for us.**

The Heart Sutra

Once all us trainees had dried off, we continued on along secret paths towards Yudono Shrine. Our vow of silence meant that we could internalise the experience, and taste it again without it being diluted or distorted by anyone else's recounting of theirs. I found my mind wandering to the births of my children, most likely led there by the terrific sound of water, which still rang in my ears.

When I became a mother, my firstborn arrived in the middle of a dramatic winter storm. My second arrived only eighteen months later, just as I entered midlife and had a meltdown which led to writing books.

The entire force of the universe had coursed through my veins as I brought new life into the world, standing at the edge of the portal, ushering my babies in. I had a similar experience birthing my first book. This year, I approached the portal again, as I ushered my mother back through it. On every occasion both destruction and creation were present. The world before and after. My perception of that world before and after. Daily life before and after. But not once, until my mum died, did I give myself any kind of real grace period, enough time to adjust properly to this new world situation I found myself in, and to take in the enormity of what had just happened. There was simply too much to be done.

As I climbed up towards Yudono Shrine, recalling each of these huge ruptures in my life in turn, Date Masamune's death poem came floating back to me: '*I survived the darkness of this fleeting world guided only by the bright moon in my heart*' [written *kokoro* in the original poem].[2] Perhaps that is how we can best navigate life transitions such as midlife too, knowing that there will be darkness, because there is grief – if simply from the awareness that nothing lasts for ever – but that we are always guided by the light of the bright moon in the *kokoro*.

It is only while I was thinking about this that I made the connection to the Heart Sutra, which we had been chanting numerous times a day on each of Dewa Sanzan's sacred mountains, and which the monks were chanting at Eiheiji's dawn prayers back in the autumn. According to Alex Kerr, author of

Finding the Heart Sutra, it 'teaches that in the end there's nothing outside ourselves that we may cling on to. This realization, which might seem rather bleak, can also be a source of strength.'[3] It is the principle of relying on your own *kokoro* for guidance and stability in an unpredictable world.

It is no coincidence that I have been my most emotional at those turning points of birth and death. The *kokoro* is a sensitivity chamber, and when our edges are burnt away by the elemental powers of creation and destruction, there are no barriers. It can feel everything.

This does not just happen at the time of a physical birth or death. It happens at the point of any trajectory-shifting event we might experience during our lives, which involves a before and an after. We have many occasions for rebirth during our time as a human being. And with each rebirth we see anew the vastness of who we are becoming, a vastness that is necessary to take in everyone we have ever been, everyone we have loved and everyone who has loved us, as well as all the potential for every person we have yet to become.

Fearless living

The most famous line of the Heart Sutra is: '*Shiki soku ze kū, kū soku ze shiki*' (色即是空、空即是色). This translates as: 'Form is emptiness, and emptiness is form.'[4] Sometimes the word 'boundlessness' is offered as an alternative to 'emptiness'. If we, in our forms as human beings, are truly boundless, then as the Heart Sutra goes on to tell us, without hindrance, no fears exist.[5]

But here's the thing. For me, midlife has been plagued by fear, self-doubt and anxiety. You can hear them echoing in all those questions I carried with me onto Hagurosan:

- How do I know if I am doing life right? (*Read*: I am afraid I'm doing life wrong.)
- How can I be more efficient with my time? (*Read*: I am afraid I am not efficient enough, and that I am spending my time on the wrong things.)
- What should I do about money? Should I be making more money? Should I care less about money? (*Read*: I am afraid I don't have enough money, but more than that, I am afraid that not having enough money means I am not good enough.)
- How can I balance the pull to do meaningful work with the needs of my family? *(Read*: I am afraid that the truth is these things are mutually incompatible.)
- What will I regret years from now if I don't do it at this point? (*Read*: I am afraid I am missing the boat on something, without knowing what that is, which makes it even worse.)
- What if I make a choice and it is the wrong one? (*Read*: I am so afraid, I am choosing to do nothing, but I am also afraid I will regret that choice.)

This secret was so well kept that it was hidden even from me, until I was ravaged by the death of my mother. Until then I would have always said she was the worrier. Not me, oh no. I am super positive. I don't ruminate, I get on with things. Except now I see that 'getting on with things' does not mean you aren't afraid, it just means you are an expert at using action to cover up fear.

Not long after my experience on Yudonosan, I was back in Kyoto preparing for the next phase of my trip. I woke up early one morning and headed to Nanzenji,[6] a beautiful temple at the foot of the Higashiyama mountains. I had written about Nanzenji in my book *The Way of the Fearless Writer*, which had just come out in the US, and I wanted to take a photograph of it in front of the huge entrance gate known as the Sanmon, before any visitors arrived. The Sanmon has a flight of wide stone steps leading up to three rectangular doorways which frame the forested temple grounds beyond. *Sanmon* (三門) means 'three gates' and refers to the Three Gates of Liberation in Buddhism: desirelessness, formlessness and emptiness. In writing the book, I had discovered how these three 'gates' were essential for becoming a fearless writer.

I flicked through the book to the part about Nanzenji, and found that I had written this:

> The fearless writing path is actually a pathless path, unfolding with each step and leading us not from here to there, but from here to here. It is a path of waking up. Our work as fearless writers is to pass through these three gates over and over, every time we enter our sacred writing space. Shedding our fixed identity. Letting go of our desire and our need for control. Honouring the formlessness of our creative potential. Sensing the interconnectedness of everything. And practising. Always practising, to express the human condition and this strange and beautiful experience of existence, in words.
>
> The gates have no doors. They are symbolic. There is nothing stopping us from passing through. We just have to keep showing up with courage, humility and grace as we cross the threshold between the mundane and the sacred every single time we choose to write, never quite knowing what will happen next.[7]

I got full body shivers reading it. I had worked on that manuscript for months, writing and rewriting, editing and reading again. I had even recorded the audiobook version myself. And yet it wasn't until that moment at Nanzenji that I fully realised that what I had written was not just true for writing. It was also true for life.

Kokoro made visible

I am a fearless writer. I haven't always been able to say that, but writing my way through midlife, one book after another, heavily influenced by Eastern philosophy, taught me how to become one. I learnt to listen not *to* my *kokoro* as if it was separate from me, but rather to listen *from* it. It took me five years and five books to understand what it took to be a fearless writer, and yet all that time I failed to notice that being a fearless human being required exactly the same thing. But I can see it now.

My midlife malaise had shown up because *I was focused on my own desire*. I had a fixed vision of how I wanted my life to be, but got frustrated when it didn't look exactly that way. I had the kind of audacious, specific and time-bound goals we are so often told we need to have if we are going to achieve anything useful. Sometimes, I would reach one but feel uncomfortable shouting about it. Sometimes, I failed to reach one, which was not a good feeling. Other times, delivering on the timelines was not compatible with things I really valued, like time with my young family.

It was exacerbated by the fact that *I was obsessed with form*. I had a particular idea of how I thought my life *should* be by now, based on my conditioning and what I saw when scrolling through social media. This is a slippery slope, where nothing is ever enough. I was very familiar with this, having written an entire book about how perfectly imperfect we are,[8] so you'd think I'd know better, but our conditioning runs deep.

Finally, my midlife malaise had revealed the awkward truth

that *I was hostage to the idea of separateness*. I saw most people as judge, critic and competition. As a result, I rarely asked for help, or shared where I was struggling.

Being by my mother's side as she faced death, and navigating the path of grief all the way to the summit of Gassan, changed everything for me. It revealed my own patterns and showed me how important it was for me to let them die too, in order to fully live. I would rather have found out another way, without the intensity and devastation caused by the rupture, but this is where I am.

It makes complete sense that what works for writing works for life, because writing is simply a way of accessing our deepest wisdom, capturing what we have sensed about the innermost nature of things and offering our natural creative response to the world. Writing, just like any other creative act, is an instrument of the *kokoro*.

> ## It is through our creative acts that the *kokoro* is made visible.

By midlife the *kokoro* refuses to be silenced any more. This is surely why so many of us get a desperate urge to do something creative at this point. That 'something creative' has many faces – from endeavours such as art, writing, and music, to house renovation, starting a new business, conscious parenting or innovating the way we live. It's the *kokoro*'s way of seeking out new instruments to communicate our longings and deepest wisdom, and for responding to the beauty in the world.

In his bestselling novel *How Do You Live?*, Genzaburō Yoshino wrote: 'The first, most basic step is to start with the moments of real feeling in your life, when your heart is truly moved, and to think about the meaning of those. The things that you feel most deeply, from the very bottom of your heart, will never deceive you in the slightest ... That is what is most important, now and always.'[9]

Time to get real

There is a famous Zen koan which asks, 'What is your original face?'[10] This is a challenge to contemplate the real you, before the grown-ups and society got involved, and the whole complicated story of your life got going.

We are born innocent of labels. If you have ever seen a newborn baby sleeping or staring into the eyes of a parent or grandparent, you will know that they are made of love and light. That is all there is before society starts to mould you. Rebirth is the return.

What we are talking about here is the most risky of human endeavours: the return to who we really are, which is who we were before we became afraid.

Such a return does not involve going backwards to some past version of ourselves. We are operating outside of linear time here, living now in accordance with the soul's wisdom. It is life lived as expression and prayer, responding to each arising moment from the *kokoro*.

This is not easy work. It is not convenient for society, nor for people who are comfortable with their fixed idea of who we are. There will be pushback, and people will put obstacles in our way. But it is essential. And we must begin today.

We do not have for ever.
Time is of the essence.

For me, the question has ceased to be one of how I'll feel when I get to the end of my life. It has become a question of how I'll feel when I get to the end of each and every day.

I will no longer worship at the temple of desire, form and separateness. This is my vow: *From now on, I will wholeheartedly devote myself to honouring longing, presence and connection, living a creative, slow and simple life, tuned in to the rhythms of the world.*

As soon as the words have fallen from my mouth, I have a flashback to sitting alone in the kitchen of my tiny Tokyo apartment more than two decades ago, flicking through a new magazine, dreaming of buying an old house in the Japanese countryside for less than my annual salary. This longing has been there all that time. Why has it taken me half my lifetime to give it real attention?

I am in a different stage of life now, with different circumstances, so the manifestation of that longing may no longer look like an old house in the Japanese countryside, but I refuse to ignore the underlying impulse towards living a slower, more simple life for one more day. Now is the time.

Gather your things, my friend, we are hitting the road again.

KOKORO WORK: RETURNING

- What creative urges have you sensed in recent years, months and weeks? What poetry lies beneath your skin? What hunger flows in your veins? What quiet dreams, and dreams of quiet, call to you across the chaos and the noise?

- How might the concepts of desirelessness, formlessness and emptiness help you release any fears you have around creative expression, in any form?
- What is your vow? What will you wholeheartedly devote yourself to from now on? Is this a new dream, or have you been carrying it for some time?

KOKORO WISDOM

A life well lived is a life fully expressed.

It is the *kokoro* that makes us human, and it is in the expression of our inner wisdom and creativity that we can share that humanness with others – both the beauty and the chaos – joining ourselves to the web of everything and reminding each other that we are not alone.

CHAPTER 10

NOURISHMENT

Goodness in. Goodness out.

'I am Little Field,' the woman said, her smile as wide as a pumpkin as she raced over to introduce herself. 'And that's the extent of my English,' she added in a strong local dialect, before bursting into laughter. Obata-san, whose name is written with characters that mean 'small' and 'field', held out a baby rosemary plant and a trowel. 'Do you want to help?' The truth was, in that moment, there was nothing I would rather do. It was mid-morning at Fujiya Farm, a kitchen garden belonging to Matsunaga Rokkan,[1] the inn across the road where I had spent the night. 'Rokkan' means 'six senses', and the inn was so named to capture its philosophy of going beyond the five bodily senses of sight, hearing, smell, taste and touch to include a felt sense of the world discovered in stillness.

Surrounded by forested low mountains in rural Fukui, we were in wild monkey country, and whole families of them scampered across the slopes. Obata-san and her colleague Itamochi-san, a gentle man my age, were good company as we spent the rest of the morning with our hands in the soil, collars up against the wind, planting herbs and pansies and tending to greenhouse crops. We picked micro-cucumbers smaller than a fingernail and radishes bigger than eggs, as well as leaves to make herb tea, which we drank with crunchy rosemary biscuits, listening to the river. A huge cricket joined us. 'Nature is like the stock of a good soup,' Itamochi-san said. 'It's the foundation that makes everything else better.'

On our tea break, Obata-san chatted about a mischievous grandchild, and Itamochi-san spoke of his move to the area several years earlier, having quit his engineering career. He wanted a *yutori no aru seikatsu*, a relaxed life with breathing space, where he could be closer to nature, and have more time for people. This had been a common theme in many of my conversations on this trip.

Taking it slow

Slow living has been a way of life in Japan for generations, rhythms set in accordance with the harvest cycle, with close attention paid to the seasons, and effort and rest both valued. But in the past 150 years, since the Meiji Restoration in 1868 ushered in a new era of politics and economics, imported ideas about happiness being related to economic growth have changed this for many people.

The consumer culture in Japan is as rampant as anywhere, as is the trend for media-saturated, always-on, busy lifestyles. Rapid infrastructure development has devastated nature in many parts of the country. Data shows stress levels are high in the workplace.[2] Japan has an ageing population and large-scale migration of young productive people towards urban areas. Millions of houses in the countryside are vacant,[3] and more than half of all municipalities in Japan are designated wholly or partially underpopulated.[4] But the flow of local migration is not only moving in one direction. There is also a quiet trend of people in their thirties and forties, particularly those with young families, moving to more rural settings, and local governments all over the country are putting efforts into encouraging this.[5] Many towns offer housing subsidies, access to accommodation through the *akiya* bank (listing of vacant houses) system, and investment in activities and tours for people wanting to try out rural living before they commit.

As someone who has long harboured a secret dream of buying an old house in the Japanese countryside, I joined one such tour in rural Kyoto.[6] I was accompanied by a minibus full of midlifers looking to prioritise a 'wealth of *kokoro*' over financial wealth, through a slower, simpler lifestyle choice, where they feel part of a community and closer to the land and the food they eat. The tour was designed to give participants a real view of life in Ayabe[7] and its surrounding villages. We were taken to several local businesses to meet people who had moved from big cities and found new jobs, or created multiple income streams for themselves. Many of them were women, whose stories left a particular impression on me.

Kashiwabara-san, who moved from Osaka to rural Kanbayashi, named her guest house 'Origin',[8] so she would never forget who she really is and why she moved to the countryside. She describes where she lives as 'a very inconvenient place with no 7-Eleven or traffic lights, but an environment which makes you *feel* your life every single day'. Kashiwabara-san also runs a part-time bakery so she can work when she wants and spend time with her young daughter at home. She told me, 'Before, I was swept along by the tide of the company, but now I am rowing the boat, going at my own pace. Sometimes, it's hard to make all your own decisions, but there is a freedom in it. When you don't have constant external stimulation, it forces you to be more creative. In the city everything cost money. Now it's like, "Shall we go for a walk to the bamboo grove?" It feels better not to spend money all the time. We have time to make things together, climb trees, go hunting for frogs under the rocks. Clearing snow is tough, though,' she laughed.

Miyazono-san, who runs Koku⁹, an organic vegan cafe, and founded a women's cooperative for organic farmers, tipped a handful of rice grains into my hand and asked me, 'Can you feel the energy? That is going to become your energy when you eat it. The life and energy in our food is connected to the life and energy in our bodies.'

Watanabe-san, a delightful woman aged ninety-six, shared how she was actively trying to keep her tiny village alive. She is one of only three remaining residents, the others being her sister, also in her nineties, and her son. Their hamlet is situated deep in the mountains, and the surrounding forest is full of horse chestnut trees, which supply the chestnuts needed for a local delicacy known as *tochimochi*, a kind of soft rice cake, which they make and sell at the local hot spring. When the family was no longer mobile enough to climb up and gather the chestnuts themselves, they saw an opportunity to engage others in sustaining the village while keeping the tradition going. Every year, they invite schoolchildren and adult volunteers from near and far to come and help gather the chestnuts, and learn how to make *tochimochi*. As Watanabe-san showed me how to peel the chestnuts and roll the pounded rice, she told me stories of the old days, when she had to walk a daily five-hour return trip through bear country to school. I think we sometimes forget, or simply don't know, how hard life has been for many of our elders, and it is good to get a reminder. In every rice cake she shaped so expertly in her wrinkled hands, I could sense Watanabe-san's determination to do what she could to share her experience, skills and knowledge with others.

And then there was Aoi-san, who had strung an old shed with huge bunches of dried herbs and flowers which she sells to restaurants, and who helps out on the family cattle farm when she's not working at the local hot spring. Her days are full, but not depleting.

Aoi-san's husband told me that his yearning for the countryside appeared after nearly two decades of city life, when he realised that for him it wasn't '*inaka ni sumitai*' but more specifically '*inaka ni kurashitai*'. They both translate as 'I want to live in the countryside' but *kurashi* is more rooted. It has a sense of really living somewhere, being present to it and building a life there, rather than it being just the place where you go to work and sleep, which is how he felt about the city. He told me, laughing, the rhythm is different – it is busy but not stressful: 'You can take a nap if you really want to, but if you nap too long you'll get eaten up by the grass.'

Of course, for some people, big city life suits them. However, what I noticed among all the people I met in the villages around Ayabe and in many other parts of rural Japan was a sense of ease and contentment, which was not just a product of the countryside setting. Their rooted lives offered them support in the shape of a community. They had consciously chosen to do less, so they could focus more on one or two things that mattered to them. They all seemed acutely aware of their environment, of the season, of the food they were cooking, eating and offering, and the value they placed on time with people that they cared about. It was a joy to be in their company.

Besides their commitment to slow and natural living, these people all have something in common, which is known in Japan as *hannō, han-X*, which translates as 'half-agriculture, half-X', the X being 'something else'. This term was coined by farmer, writer and rural lifestyle pioneer Naoki Shiomi in the mid-1990s and has been growing in popularity ever since.

'It's not about being a farmer,' Shiomi-san told me. 'It's about building a sustainable lifestyle which includes some growing – which might be cultivating a rice field, or it might be ripening tomatoes on the windowsill of your apartment – and building that out with your specific gifts and skills. Tending to something is good for us humans. It can be an important part of cultivating your own life. And you don't have do the same thing for ever. Do what is interesting for as long as it is interesting, and then weave in other things. Try to find your life's theme, and then explore different expressions of that. The crucial part is the *kumiawase*, the combination which is unique to you.'

I can see now that in different ways all of my influences on this trip, from Dōgen to Ryōkan to Bashō, to Lisa and my mother and these Japanese devotees of modern slow living, have been telling me the same thing:

Slow down so you can experience more of everything that matters.

A life that feels good on the inside

Spending time around people living so consciously made me think about all the things we take in, which our bodies have to digest. To be honest, I had been thinking about this for a while, since my mother's illness. Her tumour began where the oesophagus meets the stomach, and it had made me much more conscious of what I ate and drank, and more aware of the job the body has to do to process everything we put inside it. Of course, it's not just about food either. Our bodies and minds have to deal with all the stimuli from screens and media, the noise, the air we breathe, the energy of people and places – all of it.

Thinking about this reminded me of a recent conversation I had with my friend Seiko Mabuchi. Many moons ago, Seiko and I studied together for our Masters in Interpreting and Translation. Our chats always veer off on many tangents, and that particular time we had ended up talking about decision-making. I had asked her to explain how she arrives at a decision.

Seiko thought about it for a while and then said, 'We receive all kinds of information from the senses into our heads, just as we receive other stimuli from the outside world, like news and opinions, right? Some of that information gets accepted into the *kokoro* as feeling,' she said, tapping her chest. 'This informs our immediate response in the moment. Depending on the situation, the felt information might also be stored there in the form of emotions, which can inform our responses to the world in the future. Of course, we can also feel directly, bypassing the thinking brain altogether.'

Seiko continued, 'Over time, some of the information accepted into the heart space drops into the *hara* in the form of decisions about the future. The *hara* is the belly, or lower abdominal area, known in many Eastern traditions as a source of stability and stillness, said to be where an individual can tune in to the resonance of the universe. There is an intelligence there which may be similar to the "gut feeling" expression in English, although the *hara* is not the same as the physical organ of the gut, which is known as the *chō* (腸).

'The head, heart and belly work together with the information that comes in from the outside world, digesting and filtering it through the sieve of personal experience, stored emotions and innate wisdom.'

She added, 'In Japanese we also have the expression "*fu ni ochiru*" (腑に落ちる)', which was a phrase Master Hoshino had used several times when I had interviewed him. 'It means "(I wait and the answer) falls into my bowels". This approach is based on taking time and trusting the wisdom of the body.' Her words felt important, and I repeated them to myself.

Take time and trust the wisdom of the body.

This could not have been more different to the way I had been trying to solve my midlife malaise, going round in circles with my many questions, and getting frustrated when I could not logically figure out the answers. I later shared Seiko's thoughts with a couple of other Japanese friends and they agreed: 'Exactly, it's as if information and stimuli are digested top down. We feel in different ways in the head, the *kokoro* and the belly, and our health and state of mind are affected by all three.' Everything we take in goes so deep into our bodies and affects the functioning of every part of us, down to the decisions we make about the way that we live.

Thinking about this, it made me cringe to think how often I rush a sandwich while scrolling news websites and worrying about my to-do list as I sit at my desk. It also made me want to learn more about food as a starting point to better nourish myself and my family. Fortunately, I knew a good place to begin.

Food as ritual and devotion

'It's all about the *dashi*,' Chef Nomura said, showing me a map of Hokkaido, and pointing out the best sources of different kinds of *konbu* (kelp) that are the most vital element of soup stock in Japan.

Daisuke Nomura, owner of Sougo[10] in Roppongi, had kindly let me into his kitchen for the day, to teach me the fundamentals of his style of cooking, which is inspired by none other than Zen Master Dōgen. As one of Tokyo's leading plant-based chefs, he brings a contemporary flair to food made using principles laid down more than eight hundred years ago. Chef Nomura was born into a family of restaurateurs specialising in *shōjin ryōri*, 'devotional cuisine' or food made with 'earnest commitment', the kind of food served at many temples across Japan. He developed his career in the family's restaurant, Daigo, where he became third-generation executive chef and received two Michelin stars. He opened Sougo with the aim of offering dishes that go beyond technique or taste to share a sense of gratitude for life and for food with his guests.

Chef Nomura is a regular visitor to Eiheiji, returning to the source of the Zen principles that have shaped his own philosophy. 'Dōgen left behind a text called *Tenzo Kyōkun* ("Instructions for the Zen Cook"), which is as timeless as the instructions he gave for *zazen* meditation,' he told me.

As we chopped vegetables and stirred soup, Chef Nomura outlined the key principles of cooking according to Dōgen, many of which were surprisingly relevant as an approach to life, too: 'We need three kinds of *kokoro* when we cook. *Kishin* (喜心), the *kokoro* of delight, which reminds us of the joy of cooking and hosting. It is the *kokoro* of gratitude for what is, which finds joy in the opportunity to cook, without worrying too much about the outcome. Joy first. Then *rōshin* (老心), the old *kokoro*, which I call the *kokoro* of sincerity. The character *rō* means old age, so we can think about this as the *kokoro* of a parent, taking care to nourish our guests well regardless of who is at the table, and being sincere in what we are doing. Thirdly, we have *daishin* (大心), the great or magnanimous *kokoro*, which does not force preferences. The cook works with the ingredients they have.'

He checked the soup, then continued, 'We also need to be careful when we prepare the food. Dōgen said we should make sure everything is clean, and do the job properly, with care. In fact, he said we should handle the ingredients as if they were our own eyes.'

Chef Nomura went on to explain the five fundamental methods for preparing food in *shōjin ryōri* (raw, simmered, steamed, grilled, fried), the five colours (red, green, yellow, white, black) and the five tastes (salty, sweet, sour, bitter, hot) which chefs try to incorporate in each menu. He added that Dōgen actually defined a sixth taste, *tanmi*, as an essential taste in *shōjin ryōri*. It is hard to describe but is quite similar to *umami*, which was discovered more recently. Whereas *umami* literally means 'delicious taste' – and refers to the meaty savouriness found in things such as seaweed, mushrooms and miso, which can enhance other flavours – more than a distinct flavour itself, *tanmi* is the lightness of the food, the taste sensation of something being fresh and natural, and not overseasoned. It is thought to contribute to the feeling of satisfaction after a meal. The overall aim of these guidelines is to achieve variety and balance.

Chef Nomura went on to tell me that Dōgen also left instructions for those who eat, encouraging reflection, self-control and gratitude: 'We are encouraged to engage with our food, appreciating what someone has taken the time to prepare, considering how it got onto the plate and all those who were involved in feeding us, and offering thanks. Each mealtime is also an opportunity to reflect upon the day and upon our state of mind, and then when we tuck in, we should eat slowly and enjoy how the food is medicine for rejuvenating our bodies.'

Yet again I am stunned at how the ideas of a Zen Master from all that time ago, who lived in a completely different time to us and had access to a lot less science and other information, are still so relevant today. Food, prepared carefully from nutritious ingredients, offered with love and eaten with gratitude, can help rejuvenate and restore us. Every meal is an opportunity to let goodness in, so we have the energy to offer goodness back out.

Kokoro expression as offering

Some of the most exquisite food I have ever eaten was at Satoyama Jūjō[11], deep in the mountains of rural Niigata. A friend had recommended the place to me, and it was only when I arrived that I discovered that the restaurant, Sanaburi, is rated one of the best rural eateries in the world.

Let me give you a taste ... First up was *ayu* (river fish) gently fried with *jagaimo* (potato) and *satsumaimo* (sweet potato) chips, served on large leaves from the garden. Then raw, smoky *maguro* (tuna) with a salad of beetroot, boiled chrysanthemum and red pepper foam, followed by miso soup.

The next course, of beef, green onion, peanuts and *daikon*, made me realise how chopsticks limit how much you can take in at once, so you really appreciate the flavours. The chopstick rest was made of tied *wara* (rice straw), the same material used in the *yukimuro* hut outside, which employs a 200-year-old technique to snow-age food.

Then there was cauliflower and octopus, then more fish and spinach, then a hotpot of chicken and *shimeji* mushrooms, and rice with *okoge* (the honourable burnt bits). Dessert was a panna cotta with caramelised *daizu* soy beans, fresh *kaki* (persimmon) and roasted tea. After the meal, Head Chef Keiko Kuwakino arrived with a clear pot of mint tea to tell me more about the food and her philosophy. The restaurant's name is inspired by the ritual feasting that accompanied the annual cycle of rice planting and harvesting in Niigata long ago, and the hyper-seasonal menus are designed based on what has come in from the farmers and foragers. Originally an aesthetician, Chef Kuwakino studied Ayurveda and yoga before becoming a chef. She said, 'Changing what I do hasn't changed who I am. It's just the form of expression that has changed. My passion is still to bring people health, beauty and happiness.' At Sanaburi, Chef Kuwakino's *kokoro* is served up on a beautiful wooden plate.

One element of *kokoro* that came up over and over in my conversations was its link to a sense of *omoiyari*, consideration. This can manifest in many ways, from thoughtfulness to generosity, from hospitality to altruism. It is the sense of taking care of others, which is evident in so many interactions in Japan.

Later that night, I spent an hour in the *rotenburo*, the outdoor hot spring bath, under the stars. I gazed out towards the distant mountains, hidden by the night but clear in my imagination, thinking of home, and creating a *yutori no aru seikatsu* – a life with breathing space, where everything was done with the kind of care and attention offered up at Satoyama Jūjō.

The *Kokoro* Laundry

When I think about breathing space, it also makes me think about how stressful I find crowds of people, and how paying attention to small things like that – and avoiding crowds as far as possible – can make a huge difference to how I feel on any given day. I remember asking a taxi driver in Kyoto where he goes when the crowds get overwhelming. 'Rengeji,' he said. 'The temple is often very quiet and my *kokoro* is calm there.'

After one particularly stressful run-in with a huge group of tourists outside the famous Kiyomizudera Temple, I abandoned my plan to visit it and hailed a cab to Demachiyanagi station instead. I took the quiet Eizan railway north, alighting at the blink-and-you'll-miss-it Miyake Hachiman station.

For some reason, my phone map sent me down a back street, which I would notice later was actually the long way round. I came across two men sitting on a wooden veranda, small white raked sand garden at their feet, chatting lazily in the sun alongside an open-sided building which felt like a tiny cafe, but had no counter and was in the middle of a residential street. I called a greeting to the men, and asked what kind of place it was.

The younger of the two explained that it was not a cafe but a gathering place, and invited me in to have a look around. 'People can hire it, and strangers who are lucky enough to stumble across it can take a cold beer from the fridge for 300 yen and sit at the table for a while,' he explained. 'But mostly we just hang out here with family and friends.'

The place had a roof but no walls, and few pieces of furniture besides log stools and a 4m-long table hewn from a single piece of *keyaki* (Japanese zelkova) wood. As I was running my hand along the table admiring it, I looked up to the far end of the space and did a double take.

Hanging from the ceiling was a hand-painted wooden sign naming the place the *Kokoro no Sentaku Hoshi Bar* (with 'Bar' written in English), which could be translated as The *Kokoro* Laundry, or more specifically, the bar where you can hang out your *kokoro* to dry after you have given it a good clean. Stunned, I explained my interest in the word *kokoro* and asked why he and his father had chosen that particular name.

'For me, *kokoro* is all about the relationships between people,' he said. 'We construct walls around ourselves so the breeze cannot blow through and clear out our storehouse of emotions. Things stagnate or putrefy. Taking the time to relax with friends, to host them and share precious time with them, can help us clean our *kokoro,* which in turn helps us in those relationships.'

I stayed for a while, chatting in the shade, cooled by their laidback voices and the sound of a stream running nearby. They waved me off with an invitation to return any time, and as I stepped back out into the road I felt strangely refreshed. I carried on to Rengeji, although my stress had already been washed away at The *Kokoro* Laundry.

The taxi driver had been right. There was not another soul at Rengeji,[12] besides the monk who took my money at the entrance.

He was friendly and didn't look busy, so I asked him about *kokoro*. He thought for a moment, then replied, 'I feel something in response to the world. It's like a piece of paper rustled by the wind, the sensing of movement. That is what I call *kokoro*, but you should probably ask some other monks.'

I sat down at the edge of the large tatami room and looked out over the garden. At first, I closed my eyes, took a deep breath and

inhaled the stillness. *The pain of the past is only present if I invite it in.*
Anxiety about the future is only present if I invite it in. In this moment
of stillness my calm mind chooses nothing, except to expand its awareness
to join with nature, which is all around me. And perhaps listen out for
pieces of paper rustled by the wind.

On opening my eyes, I noticed that within the stillness of the
temple garden there was actually so much movement. Light was
weaving a pattern on a rock, tiny concentric circles drifted away
from busy minnows, giant koi carp swam slowly in the shadows,
and a small bird I didn't recognise hopped about. Butterflies
flitting, incense wafting, a dragonfly scouting for food, moss
growing more slowly than I could imagine, but growing all the
same. And me breathing even more slowly and deeply than when
I arrived.

I took out my phone to take a photo of the pond, and found
myself flicking through photos from the past year. In some I
looked my age. In others, a little younger. In a few, I looked
ninety. Viewed this way, I realised something I had never really
noticed before. Whether my skin is glowing, whether I have lines
on my face, and whether I look radiant is very little to do with my
physical age. I was pretty much the same age in all of the photos.
Rather, it's that my face reflects the state of my *kokoro*, as well as
the degree to which my skin is nourished from within. While
face masks have their place, the best beauty treatment for me is
clearly feeling good inside my days, and I sensed that for me that
means living a slower, more simple life.

A slow life is not a boring life,
it is an engaged life.

A slow life is one where we take time to nourish ourselves in every way, and find contentment in the smallest of details. I knew I wanted to feel more often like I felt there at Rengeji, like I felt at Satoyama Jūjō and in Chef Nomura's kitchen – conscious of my own need for nourishment, and giving myself permission to pay attention to that, knowing that nourishing myself would allow me to better nourish others.

And I felt that the key to doing this in a sustainable way was to not push wellness to the edges. I had to make work more nourishing too.

For a long time I had been doing work that I considered meaningful, but had never really stopped to think about the toll that it was taking on my wellbeing. It was time for a new approach, where the work became nourishment itself.

KOKORO WORK: NOURISHMENT

- How could you better nourish your body?
- How could you better nourish your relationships, and be nourished by them?
- How could you better nourish your *kokoro*?

KOKORO WISDOM

A life well lived is a life well nourished.

What we take into our bodies affects how we feel,
and what energy we have for living. When we
are conscious of what we consume, we are taking
care of our *kokoro*, and this affects our mood,
our perspective and our feelings of contentment.

CHAPTER 11

WHOLEHEARTEDNESS

The time is now

D awn at Shimoike Pond was not a quiet affair, as five thousand swans prepared for take-off. There seemed to be no order to their departure, they just went when they were ready. A lone swan, or a pair, or a small group would beat their wings and fly low across the entire width of the pond, before rising into the sky and heading off over the rice fields in search of breakfast.

As the sun slowly rose, my friend Tarō and I sat on a bench sipping mushroom tea, eating melon cake and pointing out all the ways the swans looked like humans trying something new. Some raced ahead, others swam around calmly, observing, uninterested in rushing. Some seemed to watch those taking off as if in awe, trying to sum up the courage to do it themselves, which they all eventually did.

Something from nothing

I was in Tsuruoka to interview Tarō's boss, Daisuke Yamanaka, CEO of the urban development company Yamagata Design, which owns the stunning Shōnai Hotel Suiden Terrasse[1] where I was staying. Yamanaka-san is clearly a powerhouse. I spotted him in *Monocle* magazine a while back, and in just a few short years his company has transformed the area around Tsuruoka, first with the hotel and spa and Kids Dome Sorai[2], one of the most incredible children's play facilities I have ever seen, and now with a new agriculture business. To be honest, I was a little nervous about meeting him, which is probably why it began the way it began.

'Do you sleep well?' I asked, an unusual first question for any interview, but particularly in Japan. I had meant to ask if he *ever* slept, given how many projects he had going on. Yamanaka-san burst out laughing, and the nerves evaporated. He was younger than me, whip-smart and disarmingly open with his views, some of which are quite unconventional for a Japanese CEO. (Apparently he sleeps fine, by the way.)

I asked what had brought him to Yamagata. 'I wanted to start afresh, to see if I could survive outside Tokyo. To build a life from a "zero base" [his term] and see what happened.' At the time he made such a radical decision, Yamanaka-san was rapidly climbing the career ladder at Mitsui Fudōsan, one of the largest real estate developers in Japan. 'Working at the company was safe and stable, but it was my backbone. I didn't know if I had one without the company name behind me. Even though I was still in my twenties, the older I got, the clearer it became that the price I was paying for stability was my own freedom, and I realised that my freedom was more important.' He wanted to be free to make decisions, make mistakes, make things happen, and make a life where and how he wanted.

Yamanaka-san moved to Yamagata – a place he had never been – knowing no one other than the CEO of Spiber, an innovative biotech company who had given him a job. It took him a matter of months to see the huge potential of the area, and he soon quit to found Yamagata Design, with just 100,000 yen, not much more than £500. Today, Shōnai Hotel Suiden Terrasse, designed by Shigeru Ban, the same award-winning architect who designed Zenbō Seinei, receives more than 60,000 guests a year. From the hotel's restaurant, Moon Terrasse, Gassan is visible in the distance.

Curiously, Yamanaka-san said he has no plans to create a chain of similar hotels in rice fields across the nation, even though there are huge opportunities and investors waiting in the wings. 'It's not interesting to me,' he said. 'I had an idea, wondered if it would work, and tried it out. I don't want to be a hotelier. I have other things I want to try.'

I noticed that Yamanaka-san used the word *omoshiroi*, and its opposite, *omoshirokunai*, many times in the interview. My husband recently commented how often I use the English equivalent of *omoshiroi*, 'interesting', in conversation. I hadn't noticed until he mentioned it, but it's true. I use it as a marker to acknowledge new information or something I want to explore further. I also use it in conversation to show that I am listening and would love to hear more.

Omoshiroi (面白い) is written using the characters for face or front side (面) and the colour white, like a blank piece of paper (白い). The etymological dictionary *Gogen Yurai* actually describes the breakdown of the characters as 'in front of your eyes' and something being 'bright and clear'. I love this description. To discover what we are interested in, and to stay interested in it, we just have to keep paying attention to what is clear and bright in front of our faces.

'As long as I have enough money for my children's education, for health and for good food, that's plenty,' Yamanaka-san said. 'I'm not interested in stashing money away for some day in the future. I am interested in what is possible right now, here in this place, at this point in my life, and at this moment in the world.'

'Now' is this moment in time and space.
'Now' is this life stage. 'Now' is this
point in history. Every moment offers a
new combination of these three levels of
'now', and births a new opportunity.

This particular moment in time, right here, right now, with the people in our orbit, offers a set of opportunities. The particular life stage we are in, with its particular circumstances, and our particular vault of wisdom and experience gathered up to this point, offer a set of opportunities. And the particular state of the world right now similarly offers a set of opportunities, perhaps related to the challenges of humanity, or the opportunities of emerging technology, or something else that until this particular moment we were not even aware of. There are opportunities everywhere, and it is even more exciting when you consider that the constellation of these opportunities is always changing, with each arising 'now'.

Yamanaka-san's words reminded me of Onodera-san, an inspiring woman I had met just a couple of days earlier.

The time is now

Onodera-san owns Naa[3], a wonderful organic farm-to-table restaurant in Tsuruoka, not far from Yamanaka-san's hotel. Three decades ago, aged forty, with five children under the age of eight to take care of and considerable debt to deal with, she got a cancer diagnosis that shook her awake. She believed her illness was related to her stress levels and diet, and realising that she had to stay alive for the sake of her children, she began growing vegetables in the corner of a rice field owned by her family.

Her first priority was to eat well and nourish her children, and her second was to create her own income stream so she didn't have to rely on anyone else. Onodera-san's production was as close to organic as possible, and she started selling her vegetables, doing house-to-house deliveries with the help of friends. The word spread and her business, timed as it was with a growing wave of interest in organic food, flourished. She said it was a challenging but joyful time, and she loved having her children in the fields with her.

She was telling me her story while sitting at one of the tables of a new breakfast restaurant she was just about to open, and she reminisced about how that initial success was a combination of her complete focus on what needed to be done at the time, her particular life stage, and what was happening in the world back then, with a growing trend towards healthier food. She looked around her new venture and smiled. 'It's the same now,' she said. 'I'm always up early, I want to work fewer hours, and people around here want somewhere to go for a delicious breakfast. It's perfect.' She was bringing a new expression of her *kokoro* to the now of her life stage and the now of her community's evolution.

We often think of change as a scary thing, but every time the world shifts, new opportunities open up. It is fascinating to keep checking in with our own trio of nows – what is possible and interesting to us right now (today, this month, this year), in this particular life stage, and in this particular moment in history? What does technology offer us right now that wasn't previously possible? What do people want and need because of the way the world is right now? And how do we want to be in our working lives, in this particular moment in our lives, in the particular circumstances we find ourselves in? It might be that change is afoot, but it might be that an interesting opportunity is actually bright and clear in front of our face.

The not-blank blank page

I mentioned how Yamanaka-san had talked about starting from a 'zero base', a blank sheet. I know from my own work that the idea of this is one of the scariest things for people who are looking to make a significant change in their life, but here's the thing . . . Although the two-dimensional sheet of paper on which we draw our new dreams might appear blank when we look at it face on, if we turn it to the side we can see that it is actually backed by all of our experience, all the wins, all the lessons learnt from the mistakes, all the skills we have built, connections we have made, and all the ideas we have scribbled in our journals, never mind the teachings of everyone who came before. It is all stored there in that space behind the blank sheet on which we sketch out what our longings might look like, manifested. We can reach through the page and into that space to draw on them any time we like, or we can turn the page face on, and let our imaginations go wild with the blank sheet.

At the beginning of Shunryū Suzuki's classic *Zen Mind, Beginner's Mind*, the opening page shows lettered characters in thick black strokes: 初心. Read *shoshin*, this term means 'beginner's mind'.[4] We could also say 'first heart'. It is the *kokoro* of the enthusiastic beginner with a heart full of possibilities.

> **To have a beginner's mind is to be willing to be reborn over and over, eyes open and curious about the world.**

Every moment, every day, every new project and every new opportunity invites us to approach it with a beginner's mind, in the knowledge that we stand upon everything that has gone before – all of our experience, resources, connections, lessons learnt from mistakes made, and all the rest of it. Nothing is wasted. Everything leads somewhere, even if we don't yet know where.

The relief of 'whatever'

I asked Yamanaka-san about his approach to decision-making. 'There are so many things in life we could be doing, how do you decide which ones you should be doing?' He shared three words that guide him: *suki* (like), *kirai* (dislike) and *mendō kusai*. It was my turn to laugh. *Mendō kusai* means 'it stinks of effort'.

'Seriously,' he said. 'It's not about like or dislike in terms of taste, but in terms of feeling. If I don't like something, I don't keep doing it. If something feels good – if I like it – I do more of it. If I stop liking it, I stop doing it and do something else. And if it is *mendō kusai*, if it stinks of effort, I don't do it either. I go for ease.' It sounds so obvious when he says it, and yet it is a complete revelation.

'Oh, there's one more,' he said. '*Dō demo ī.*' I was not expecting that. *Dō demo ī* means 'whatever', or 'I don't really care'. 'Don't get me wrong,' he added quickly. 'I do my absolute best on projects I'm committed to, but over the years I have wasted so much time going over and over things in my head when I have made a mistake or if I am worried about something, that I have come to understand that, in the end, nothing really matters that much. It saves so much stress. Do your best, and then let that be good enough.'

Talking to Yamanaka-san was like having a long cool drink on a hot day. I was curious about what kind of a boss he was. He told me, 'When we started out, Yamagata Design was a mission-driven company, totally focused on building the area as a great place to live and work. It had to be. It was the only way to get sufficient buy-in for the kinds of things we wanted to do. It takes a huge team effort to pull off something like this. But over the years, I have realised that if you are too mission-focused, the mission can actually become a reason that you get caught up in projects that you personally aren't interested in and, to me, that is not sustainable. So now we are a company that prioritises employee happiness. I will be boss for as long as I, and everyone who works here, loves their job. When that stops, it's time for me to go and do something else.'

Onodera-san and Yamanaka-san were two of many inspiring people I met who live in the shadow of the three sacred mountains of Dewa, going about their lives with intention and managing to conform to expected ways of being in community, without conforming to the stereotypical fixed career path that many of us might associate with Japan. In every case it was clear that no one has forged their path alone, and that the people they have around them have made a huge difference to what they have been able to do.

> It isn't just having a support network that matters, but having the *right* support network. That changes everything.

At the end of the interview, Yamanaka-san reflected, 'I want to die well', by which he meant he wanted to have squeezed all the juice out of life, and go when he was ready. It was another way of saying he wanted a life well lived, but there was something about his use of the verb 'to die' that subtly changed the focus. He wanted to die with no regrets, having not wasted his life on things he didn't like, or which stank of effort. Permission granted, and an inspiration for us all.

KOKORO WORK: WHOLEHEARTEDNESS

- What opportunities are presenting themselves to you right now? What is possible because of this particular moment, life stage and time in history?
- What would you love to give your wholehearted effort and attention to? What is stopping you? What step could you take in the direction of making that possible?
- What do you currently do that stinks of effort? How could you do things differently to invite more ease?

心

KOKORO WISDOM

**A life well lived is an unfolding path
paved with what feels right.**

The language of the *kokoro* is spoken in energetic impulses which we feel in our bodies. We can sense when something is right or not right, feels good or does not feel good. When we navigate life this way, tuning in to this wisdom instead of being buffeted by external influences, we walk a path which feels right for us.

CHAPTER 12

INTENTIONALITY

We get to have this day

T he inkiest part of night had begun to fade. The first *horagai* had sounded a short while earlier, and this time I had been ready to move. I pulled on my *shiroshozoku*, did up the *jika tabi* boots that I was becoming quite fond of, grabbed my wooden staff from where it leant against the outdoor toilet block and took my place in line one last time.

Without a word, or any hint of breakfast, we set off out of the pilgrim lodge, down the road and straight up the 2,446 uneven stone steps of Hagurosan. We bowed at Jijisugi, the Grandpa Cedar, chanted in the shadow of the five-storeyed pagoda, and paused to repeat the Heart Sutra at some of the many shrines along the mountain path. I felt strong all the way.

As the sun rose, I thought about all that had happened since I had last climbed those same steps in my clunky walking boots the previous autumn, shortly after Lisa's cremation, before I had any inkling about my mum being ill. I thought of how my quest in search of the *kokoro* had been a perfect storm of midlife, loss and grief on many levels, and yet it had also been joyful, inspiring and filled with beauty in so many ways.

In my forty-six years on earth I had never cried so much, nor laughed so much, in a single year. I acknowledged the physical, mental and emotional challenges, which had reminded me that engaging the rational mind is not the only way to experience to the world, make decisions or sense what truly matters.

I thought of the hundreds of precious conversations I had been gifted about life transitions, death and living well, and how it seemed to me that our *kokoro* not only gives us access to our own wisdom, but surely carries traces of the wisdom of everyone we have ever encountered, that of our ancestors and of the earth herself.

I was so deep in this reflection and prayer of gratitude that I was surprised when the *horagai* sounded our arrival at the top of the mountain.

We lined up behind Master Hoshino in front of Hagurosan Hachiko Jinja, the shrine of Prince Hachiko. It houses the imperial tomb of the fleeing prince who followed the *yatagarasu*, the mystical three-legged crow, here to Dewa Sanzan and opened the mountains as a centre of nature worship more than fourteen hundred years ago. As we chanted the Heart Sutra one more time I felt a rush of gratitude towards the entombed prince, to my guides and to the three sacred mountains of Dewa, which had called to me over the ocean and led me deep into my inner life, held me as I burnt, composted the ash of my edges, and offered me the chance of rebirth.

We took part in a special secret ceremony at the main shrine, an imposing red building with an immense thatched roof – the largest in all of Japan. When we exited we passed the mirror pool, a ten-ton bell and a monument known as the Peace Tower, a perfectly smooth stone sphere, crowned with a small statue of a black crow with three legs. The *yatagarasu*, at rest now.

As we flew down the mountain I felt an unfamiliar lightness, and sensed how the inner spaciousness that had begun to open up on Hagurosan the previous autumn had expanded infinitely over the course of the toughest year of my life, and brought with it the realisation that I can create the life I want, step by step, day by day.

Contemplating legacy

Returning to Kyoto to tie up a few loose ends, I had the feeling of an ending approaching. There was one last place I wanted to go. I hailed a taxi for Shōrenin,[1] the temple I wrote about at the beginning of my earlier book, *Wabi Sabi*. The driver, Mr Onishi, asked me what I was doing in Japan, and somehow we got onto the topic of legacy. 'I'm not going to leave my children anything,' he said. 'I'd rather spend it enjoying the time I have with them and their children. Besides, it's more valuable for them to work things out for themselves.' It was an unusual take on legacy, but a thought-provoking one.

You might remember that at the beginning of this journey I was locked in a battle with myself. My ego wanted to be in control, have a plan and make it happen, be successful in the eyes of others, and build enough wealth to leave a substantial legacy when I'm gone. But an inner whisper told me that what I really needed was to let go of the desire for control, stop clinging to plans, be awake to the experience of life as it unfolds, thrive in my own eyes, and live in a way which creates a legacy in the impact I have on others each and every day. Oh, and to have more fun.

I can see now that the inner whisper was a prompt from my *kokoro*, a regular reminder that appeared in the form of a fizz or a spark or a flutter when I was utterly present, experiencing joy or connection in a particular moment. The impulse told me: *This is it*. My entire family belly laughing together. *This is it*. Hugging sadness away. *This is it*. Reading a poetry book in bed with a cup of tea on a Sunday morning, utterly contented. *This is it*. Sensing a new friendship blooming. *This is it*. Knowing that something I wrote made someone else feel less alone. *This is it*. Looking up at the stars and feeling a sense of awe. *This is it*.

I can also see that my old needs for control, external validation and the building of monetary wealth were connected to beliefs about success and safety which have been worn away by the events of the past year. While I managed to let many of the things I carry die on the mountain, half a lifetime of conditioning takes a while to untangle. I suspect that my beliefs are not gone entirely, but I am slowly testing out new ways of being and responding to the world which offer the chance to shape new beliefs.

Soon it will be the end of this particular journey, and the beginning of the rest of our lives. To echo Professor Hiroi's words in the Foreword of this book, we are entering a time of transition, where our very existence depends on a shift from material growth to spiritual growth. Our approach to life has ramifications for the future of human society. It is essential that we think about how to live, individually and collectively, in order that we may make the most of our lives, and make choices which benefit humanity and nature far beyond our own existence.

When I think about the kind of legacy I want to leave behind, instead of thinking about the size of the estate I will leave to be distributed after I have gone, I am now thinking instead about different things:

- Have I taught my daughters how to lose me one day, but have me close always?
- What traces of my *kokoro* will be left behind, woven into those who survive me?
- What will have become possible, or be true or good in the world, because I lived?
- What kind of a parent, friend, mentor and community member will I have been?
- What kind of an elder will I have been, if I get the chance?
- What kind of an ancestor will I have become?

Answering these questions is a life's work. The work of the *kokoro*.

The rest of my life's work. My daily *kokoro* work, for the rest of my life. And the work that will guide my intention from now on, as I go about my daily life as a human, being.

Five kinds of *kokoro*

Mr Onishi pulled up outside Shōrenin, and as soon as I got out, I felt a flood of emotion. I remembered going there one cold December night six years earlier, at a time when I was grappling with the concept of *wabi sabi* and knowing that I had to write a sample chapter to go in my book proposal. I didn't yet know how to explain the term, but I knew it mattered. I didn't know if I'd find the right words, or if a publisher would take a risk on it. Everything was unknown.

I had cycled there, breath visible on the evening air, to see the gardens illuminated. I had picked up a fallen *momiji* leaf, blushing burgundy and curling at the edges, and felt a space in my heart open up. Right then, I had everything I needed. I felt quiet contentment, tinged with melancholy in the knowledge that such a fleeting moment would never return. In that instant, I understood something about *wabi sabi* that led the way in to the rest of the book.

I had no idea where my book *Wabi Sabi* would lead me once it left my hands and went out into the world, and I certainly did not expect it to take me on a new quest – this quest, our quest – but it did. And that's how it works. I knew the concept of *wabi sabi* mattered before I knew what it was. I knew the *kokoro* mattered before I truly knew what it was. And the reason I knew was that the wisdom was already there in my *kokoro* itself. I felt the knowing before I understood the knowing, and trusted it enough to see where it led.

Returning to Shōrenin on the fifth anniversary of the publication of *Wabi Sabi*, and reflecting on this, I realised the unfinished part of the story that had bothered me since I submitted that book all those years ago.

Wabi sabi is fundamental to the aesthetic sense and gentle nature of Japanese people. It is a worldview that guides the way they experience life, although it is rarely discussed. Its influence is everywhere, and yet it is nowhere to be seen. *Wabi sabi* is a felt response to beauty that reflects the true nature of life. It is a recognition of the gifts of simple, slow and natural living, and it is an acceptance and appreciation of the impermanent, imperfect and incomplete nature of everything. What I realise now that I did not realise then is that *wabi sabi* is a response of the *kokoro*.

When we experience a perfect moment in an imperfect world, the *kokoro* is fully engaged, sensing everything, which is why time seems to slow and hover. In such moments, it is the *kokoro* that sends us the felt impulse that we read as: *This is it. This is what it's all about.* Life, unfolding, here and now, as observed from inside the moment.

This is it. Life spoken in the language of the *kokoro*.

It took another five years of midlife storms before I realised I had already spoken of the *kokoro*, without naming it, and that naming it was the final piece of the puzzle. The happening came first and the label came later. Our job is to recognise the happening, to trust in it and follow where it leads us, even while we don't yet have the label.

I got up to leave Shōrenin, and walked quietly across a room full of tatami mats towards the exit. A framed set of words written in flowing calligraphy caught my eye. I had never noticed it before, although I would learn later it had been hanging there for at least as long as I have been alive. It said:

> *The five* kokoro *of everyday life*
>
> *The amenable* kokoro *that says, 'Yes, sure.'*
> *The reflective* kokoro *that says, 'I am sorry.'*
> *The dedicated* kokoro *that says, 'I will do it.'*
> *The humble* kokoro *that says, 'It was possible*
> *because of you.'*
> *The appreciative* kokoro *that says, 'Thank you.'*[2]

I loved the generosity of these suggestions, which acknowledge the fact that when we live, we do so in company and in community. I was beginning to learn how to accommodate others, but not at the expense of my own longing, and how to rely on my own wisdom, while asking for help when I need it. Perhaps most important of all, I was remembering what the ninety-nine-year-old nun Jakuchō Setouchi had said:

To live is to love.

Coming home

It is autumn now, and I am back in England. I am waiting on a delivery of white daffodil and pale pink tulip bulbs to plant with my children around the swing seat where we like to sit and think about my mum. Yesterday, we baked an apple crumble with the last of the apples from our tree.

This morning, I greeted the autumnal equinox at dawn, wearing some ankle warmers my mum knitted. I was sitting on a bench by the river with a mug of tea and some ginger cake, as a flock of geese passed overhead in perfect V-formation. The sky was the palest of blues, with the silhouette of a single tree like an ink splash on the hill behind. I thought about all the people we have encountered on our journey through Japan over the past year, many of whom will be observing Ohigan, 'the Other Shore', this week. This seven-day Buddhist festival is a time of remembrance, and of personal reflection.

Lisa died a year ago this week. Her husband wrote on Facebook of all the lasts he has noticed lately, like when their son put on the last t-shirt she had folded, and how the last bottle of fragrance she bought him had run out on the anniversary of her death, of all days. He is a remarkable man and his sadness was not for these tiny reminders of her, but for the fact that one day they too may fade away.

So much can happen in a year, in a lifetime, in a day. Even after all this contemplation of time – linear time, seasonal time, Dōgen's time – it is still a strange, unfathomable thing. Time expands and shrinks depending on the intensity of our activity, and seems to be suspended completely in moments of devastation and in moments of bliss. But mostly the world keeps turning, the sun and moon keep rising, and life goes on, while our sorrow and joy and hope and memories live on too.

Our grief goes on. The alchemising of our grief and loss goes on. Our unfolding, unbecoming, returning, goes on. I'm not done shedding ash, slowing, listening. This is also *kokoro* work. Part of my life's work. And tending to it is the ultimate self-care.

The past year hasn't made me stronger, it has just made me realise that I was already stronger than I knew. The taller I stood in my vulnerability, the longer the shadow of strength that fell behind me.

Grief. *Shōshin* (傷心). The scarred *kokoro*. The gaping wound might heal, but the scar remains. My scar is in the shape of those words my mother inscribed on my *kokoro* at the hospice: *We get to have this day.*

I am still in midlife. I still feel *hikikomogomo*, the bittersweetness of joy and sorrow in my heart. I still go to tell my mother news of my children and then remember all over again. But this year, and this journey with you, and the exposure to all kinds of wisdom and kindness along the way have changed me for sure. I can see that it is an honour to carry such grief, to have been loved by someone and to love them so much that their loss was unleashed with so much power.

When I was sixteen and left my school to go to sixth-form college, we made a yearbook. Beneath our photo and our name we had to share our finest words of wisdom. I wrote six words: *Life is what you make it.* A few years later I would encounter an interpretation of Dōgen's thirteenth-century teachings which said, 'Life is what I am making it, and I am what life is making me.'[3]

I was shocked and thrilled that they were so similar. It is only since I have been battered about by midlife that I have noticed the second part of Dōgen's sentence, which was missing from my yearbook quote, and which I had conveniently ignored until now: *I am what life is making me.*

We have agency, but we are not in control. We have to take risks, and love deeply, and soak up the sweetness of life wherever we can, because we never know how long we have. The only thing we know for sure, in any given moment, is this:

We are here. We are alive.
We are the lucky ones.

Each morning we wake up we have the chance to remind ourselves, 'I get to have this day.' We don't know how many more times we will get to do this. Maybe thousands, maybe just hundreds, maybe only a few more times.

Doing-time or being-time. Wasting time or making time. We get to choose.

I know what I'm choosing. More love. More laughter. More life lived in the awareness of the wildness and magnificence of all of it, right here, right now. How about you?

Time, unravelled

My old boots have taken me down to the river, drawn there by the spirit of autumn. I have a blanket around my shoulders, hot tea in a flask and Xavier Rudd in my ears. He is singing of an ancient moon and all it has been drawing from him.[4] The heartbeat of his unborn son pulsates through the song.

His haunting refrain, 'Please remember me', calls through the trees like the voices of our ancestors, my grandmother and mother, Lisa and all those we have ever lost. *Please remember me.* I stand firm on the earth, throw my arms up towards the sky and vow to never forget them.

I am singing too now, filling the sky with his song: *Please remember me.* I am swaying like the water reeds, tears tumbling down my face and I hear my own voice: *Please remember me.*

It is in remembering all who have gone before that we remember ourselves. Our original face before we were born. Our place in the woven web of everything, here because of everything and everyone who went before. Connected to everything and everyone who ever will be. We belong right here, right now, in the middle of all of it.

The moon is edging up into the night. It's a huge harvest supermoon, glowing yellow-orange in the darkening sky. As I stare, a thin cloud moves across it, rendering it blurry at the edges.

It looks just like the golden sphere in my dream.

Finally, I understand.

> *The golden sphere is time.*
> *It is the pulsating energy of a moment, holding all of the*
>   *past and all of the potential for the future.*
> *It is the heartbeat of the world.*
>
> *The golden sphere is the* kokoro.
> *It is the pulsating energy of the soul, holding all past*
>   *versions of ourselves and all our potential for*
>   *the future.*
> *It is the heartbeat of our very existence.*
>
> *The golden sphere is us, living fully.*
> *It is the manifestation of present awareness, when we take*
>   *in the light of the world and send our own light*
>   *beaming back out.*
> *It is the essence of our aliveness.*

The whisper I had heard in the Buddha Hall at Eiheiji comes floating back: 'All you need to know is right here. The rest is commentary.'

No one knows for sure what happens when we die, but until that point, we do know this:

> *For as long as we are alive, we will continue to change.*
> *Let this remind us that we can always begin again.*

> *For as long as we are alive, we have a* kokoro *to help us*
>   *sense the darkness and the beauty in the world, and*
>   *respond with creative expression, empathy and love.*
> *Let the* kokoro *be our guide.*

For as long as we are alive, we have time.
Let's live it well.

KOKORO WORK: INTENTIONALITY

- What and who do you care about, really?
- Which questions are alive in you right now?
- How will you go about your days to ensure that yours is a life well lived?

๑

KOKORO WISDOM

A life well lived is an intentional life, lived fully and in gratitude.

When we live guided by our *kokoro*, we experience a connected, meaningful life of intention, we make the most of the opportunities life presents to us, and we live in gratitude for every single day.

Epilogue

'Any dreams?' he asks, raising the blinds to take in a new day.

'Not this time,' I say. 'Slept like a newborn.'

'Cup of tea?' he offers.

'Thanks, but I'm going for a walk.'

I pull on my coat and head out into the morning while the sky is still pale pink. Up the road I go, along a wooded track and past a hedgerow bursting with fat blackberries. A tiny robin hops between the brambles, then flies over to a five-bar gate.

I follow the robin to take in the view over distant fields, and notice a single droplet of dew hanging from the gate. It is a perfect sphere, suspended. I lean in close and can see the reflection of my face, life story lines written across it, and behind me the sky and the rising sun and the promise of a new day.

The whole universe in a dewdrop, right here, right now.

Anatomy of the *kokoro*

As someone with a keen interest in translation, I have long been fascinated by the way *kokoro* is rendered in English, in literature and in poetry, on signage and websites. Besides 'heart', it also regularly appears as 'mind', 'heart-mind' and 'spirit'. For me, as someone whose native language clearly distinguishes between heart, mind and spirit, each translation has always felt more like a finger pointing at the moon, rather than being the moon itself. The fascination lies not in the fact that the word means each of those things, but, rather, that it means *all* of them, capturing a perspective very different from the one I grew up with.

At its most simple, *kokoro* means 'heart' in the widest, deepest sense of the word, and yet it does not just refer to feelings and emotions, but also to a thinking response to the world – the *kokoro* is the source of the expressive instinct in each of us. Japan's most popular dictionary, *Kōjien*, begins a long list of definitions of *kokoro* with 'the origin of a human's spiritual actions, or those actions themselves'.[1] In *The Concise Oxford Dictionary of World Religions* it is explained as 'the fundamental and interior nature of a person, thus virtually equivalent to Buddha-nature'.[2]

THE MANY FACES OF *KOKORO*

Sometimes the best way to get a sense of a Japanese character is to see how it is used in combination with others. The character for *kokoro*, 心 (often read as *shin*), appears in more than eight hundred words in the Japanese language, each of them giving a flavour of its meaning. Here are some of my favourites:

- 旅心 (*tabigokoro*), lit. travel *kokoro*: wanderlust
- 里心 (*satogokoro*), lit. hometown *kokoro*: homesickness; nostalgia
- 仏心 (*hotokegokoro*), lit. Buddha *kokoro*: mercy; charity
- 心静か (*kokoro shizuka*), lit. *kokoro*-quiet: serene; tranquil mind
- 心がおどる (*kokoro ga odoru*), lit. the *kokoro* dances: to feel buoyant, to be excited
- 熱心 (*nesshin*), lit. hot *kokoro*: zeal; enthusiasm
- 良心 (*ryōshin*), lit. good *kokoro*: conscience
- 好奇心 (*kōkishin*), lit. the *kokoro* which is fond of the unconventional: curiosity
- 本心 (*honshin*), lit. source-*kokoro*: true feelings
- 心酔 (*shinsui*), lit. *kokoro* drunkenness: adoration
- 心願 (*shingan*), lit. *kokoro* wish: prayer
- 心臓 (*shinzō*), lit. *kokoro*-internal organ: the organ of the heart
- 残心 (*zanshin*), lit. left over *kokoro*: continued alertness; follow-through (e.g. in archery and martial arts)

There are also many that reflect the shadow side of the word including:

- 賊心 (*zokushin*), lit. the *kokoro* of a thief/traitor: malicious intent
- 疑心 (*gishin*), lit. doubting *kokoro*: suspicion; apprehension
- 心労 (*shinrō*), lit. *kokoro* toil: anxiety; fear
- 心配 (*shinpai*), lit. *kokoro* distribution: worry
- 苦心談 (*kushindan*), lit. suffering-*kokoro*-talk: account of the hardships one has encountered

The word '*kokoro*' incorporates spiritual, emotional and thinking elements of a human being, and it follows that the character 心 takes in a wide range of meanings related to feelings, thoughts and emotions. The challenge is to cast aside any assumptions about the separateness of those elements and to focus instead on understanding the relationship between them. Depending on the context, *kokoro* can have a nuance of emotional or mental state, intention, empathy, wisdom or essence, or more practically signify the centre, nucleus or core of something.

The term *kokoro* has long been important in traditional culture. In Noh theatre, for example, playwright Zeami Motokiyo (1363–1443) described *yūgen*, a profound beauty which is fully felt but only glimpsed by the viewer, as a 'refined, elegant tranquil beauty of form created by means of the actor's *kokoro*'.[3] The *Routledge Encyclopedia of Philosophy* elaborates on this, saying: '*Kokoro* signifies simultaneously the emotional capacity of the artist to respond to the natural world, which ideally catalyses the act of creation; the parallel ability of an audience to respond to such a work of art and thus indirectly to the experience of the artist; and finally the evaluation of such a work as possessing the "right conception", *kokoro ari* or alternatively *ushin* [meaning "having *kokoro*"].'[4]

Fifteenth-century Tea Master Murata Shukō wrote a letter illuminating the ritual of tea as a lived expression of the inner life. The essay, which encourages the pursuit of everyday beauty, was called '*Kokoro no fumi*' – 'Letter of the Heart'.

Some three centuries later, the scholar Motoori Norinaga suggested that *mono no aware,* a sensitivity to the impermanence of all things, is both the motive and value of all literary art. This sensitivity is the *kokoro*'s response to the world.[5]

With wide usage in slogans, advertisements and song lyrics, the term *kokoro* still permeates life in Japan. Just recently, at my favourite bookstore I found a huge stack of books with *kokoro* in the title, ranging from self-help books to essay collections, from management strategy to interior design.

Kokoro is also connected to a sense of *omoiyari*, thoughtfulness and care for others. This was evidenced on a poster displayed in a public bathroom, encouraging visitors to have a 'barrier-free *kokoro*' when it came to considering the various needs of others who use the facilities.

Waiting for a train one day, I noticed a poster for a suicide prevention charity with the caption '*Kokoro ni kasa o*', offering 'an umbrella for the *kokoro*'. The poster said: 'When the rain of sadness keeps falling in your *kokoro* and things are painful and difficult, please call us.'

In contrast, the leaflet that came tucked inside my new Sunny Log Note journal, full of tips for making the most of its layout, offered this: 'Pause a moment and look up to the sky. Capture changes in the world around you, things you notice, and sparks of inspiration, so you don't miss them or forget them. (With this journal) your head will always be clear, your *kokoro* light and your outlook bright.'

When I began asking individual people about *kokoro*, I soon realised that despite its prolific usage, native speakers of Japanese found it almost impossible to articulate exactly what *kokoro* is. When I asked several people at once, unusually heated debates would erupt. Without exception, in every one of the countless conversations I have had about it, each person has offered a different explanation of *kokoro*, often using imagery instead of specifics to capture what it means to them. While a single definition may not exist, one thing did emerge with absolute clarity: *kokoro* is at once untranslatable and essential to an awakened, felt experience of the world.

The *kokoro* is a mechanism for accessing the soul's intelligence and our deepest wisdom. It is the source of our innate capacity for feeling the innermost nature of things (which join us to each other and the world we live in), as well as the source of our natural creative response to the world. It is how we see, respond to and create beauty.

The *kokoro* is the heart which thinks and the mind which feels. Some say it is the seat of the soul. To use the word *kokoro* instead of simply translating it as 'heart', 'mind' or 'spirit' as often happens, is to remind us that it is *all* of those things, the spiritual part of a human being which is imbued with a deep inner wisdom.

In many instances the word *kokoro* is used in relation to the term *tamashī*, which means 'soul' in the sense of being the spiritual part of a human being. Regardless of our personal beliefs about the existence of the soul as a separate part of the human which may or may not survive death, it is essential to be open to Japanese ideas about the existence of the *tamashī* in order to fully appreciate the influence of the *kokoro* on a human life, as understood in Japanese culture.

The *kokoro* is the internal place from which a human responds to the world in felt impulses rather than rational thought, and in

Japanese culture it is absolutely vital in navigating relationships, sensing beauty and responding to the world moment to moment. It can help us navigate life through the language of feeling, responding to the present instead of being pulled into the past or future by the regrets or worries of the monkey mind, or being pulled onto a different path by the expectations and opinions of others. The *kokoro* is also the source of the expressive instinct in each of us.

Many Japanese people I spoke to mentioned *kokoromochi*, the 'holding' of the *kokoro*, which refers to attitude, a kind of emotional mindset. Depending on the way you hold your *kokoro*, it affects your mood, which can in turn affect the moods of others. Taking care of your *kokoro*, by 'cleaning' it in the ways discussed in this book, can lift your mood and give you the feeling of carrying a happy heart.

Many native speakers of Japanese I have spoken to about the locus of the *kokoro* have indicated that it resides in the heart space. Others have suggested that it actually resides in the *hara*, the belly or lower abdomen. One person told me that they felt the *kokoro* was located in the blood, and a number felt that it was nowhere in the body, but rather everywhere, all around.

It can be disorienting not to get a universal answer to such a straightforward question, but let it not distract us from the point: the *kokoro* plays an essential part in our experiencing of the world, and responding sensitively to it.

The light of the *kokoro* guides us
along an authentic life path.

Notes

A note on the use of Japanese

1. The character 羽, which forms the 'Ha' of 'Hagurosan', means both 'wing' and 'feather'. Source: Halpern, Jack, (ed.), *NTC's New Japanese-English Character Dictionary* (Tokyo: NTC, 1993), p.129.
2. There is no formal translation into English of 'Yudonosan'. In some cases it has been translated as 'Bath Mountain' but on consultation with a local interpreter I settled on 'Sacred Spring Mountain'.
3. Zen Master Eihei Dōgen, or Zen Master Dōgen of Eiheiji, is also often referred to as Dōgen Kigen.

Foreword

1. 'Jōmon times' refers to the period from roughly 10,500–300 BCE. See the excellent essay at https://www.metmuseum.org/toah/hd/jomo/hd_jomo.htm for more details.

CHAPTER 1

1. Source: https://timbunting.com/home/yamabushi/ Retrieved September 1, 2023.
2. Based on personal correspondence with the Office of National Statistics.

3. This is based on the haiku by Matsuo Bashō which reads *arigata ya / yuki o kaorasu / kaze no oto*. Source: Matsuo, Bashō, (trans. Reichhold, Jane) *Basho: The Complete Haiku* (New York: Kodansha, 2008), p.324. There are numerous translations, some of which speak of scented snow, the faint aroma of snow, or the idea of the snow giving scent to the wind.

4. Source: Marinucci, Lorenzo, 'Hibiki and nioi. A study of resonance in Japanese aesthetics'. Article available at https://journals.mimesisedizioni.it/index.php/studi-di-estetica/article/view/879 Retrieved July 7, 2022.

CHAPTER 2

1. According to the Japan Kanji Museum & Library, Kyoto, Japan.

2. Source: Shinmura, Izuru, *Kōjien daigohan* (Tokyo: Iwanami Shoten, 1998), p.950. (Translation my own.)

3. Source: https://www.oxfordreference.com/display/10.1093/oi/authority.20110803100041699;jsessionid=4F0531ABCA3FBF27EA77167B70862598 Retrieved September 4, 2023.

4. Find out more about the Kawamura Noh Theatre at noh-plus.com

5. Source: Pilgrim, Richard B., 'Some Aspects of Kokoro in Zeami' in *Monumenta Nipponica,* Vol. 24, No. 4 (Tokyo: Sophia University, 1969), pp.393–491. Available at: https://www.jstor.org/stable/2383880 Retrieved September 1, 2023.

6. Ibid.

7. Find out more at thegooddayvelo.com

8. *Momiji* is the Japanese name for Acer palmatum, sometimes known as the Japanese maple or Japanese acer tree. It is also used as a general term to refer to fall foliage.

CHAPTER 3

1. This is from a poem written by Ryōkan Taigu upon hearing that a classmate had passed away. An alternative translation 'Life, less than a hundred years, / floats like a boat midstream' with background notes can be found in Tanahashi, Kazuaki, *Sky Above,*

Great Wind: The Life and Poetry of Zen Master Ryokan (Boulder: Shambhala, 2012), p.106.

2. Gogōan is located in the grounds of Kokujōji Temple in Tsubame, Niigata.

3. O'Connor, Tonen, 'Unfettered by Expectation', in Okumura, Shōhaku, *Ryōkan Interpreted* (Bloomington: Dōgen Institute, 2021), p.9.

4. 'No news of the affairs of men' is a reference to one of Ryōkan's untitled poems found in Stevens, John, *One Robe, One Bowl: The Zen Poetry of Ryōkan* (Boulder: Shambhala, 2006), p.43.

5. 'A monkey crying deep in the mountains' is a reference to one of Ryōkan's untitled poems found in Stevens, John, *One Robe, One Bowl: The Zen Poetry of Ryōkan* (Boulder: Shambhala, 2006), p.29.

6. Nakano, Kōji, (trans. Winters Carpenter, Juliet), *Words To Live By: Japanese Classics for our Time* (Tokyo: Japan Publishing Industry Foundation for Culture, 2018), p.24 and p.31.

7. Find out more at bio-leadership.org

8. Translation my own. Source: https://ameblo.jp/wtpwtpwtpw/ entry-12200067090.html Retrieved September 1, 2023.

9. Translation my own. Shinoda, Tōkō, *Hyaku san sai ni natte wakatta koto* (Tokyo: Gentōsha, 2017), referenced in ibid.

10. Claudel, Matthew, *Ma: Foundations for the Relationship of Space-Time to Japanese Architecture* (New Haven: University of Yale, MA thesis, 2012), p.3.

11. Translation my own. Original source: Kurose, Kikuko, *Kokoro ni naru oto* (Tokyo: Bungeisha, 2022), p.109.

12. Find out more at zenbo-seinei.com

13. Iyengar, B.K.S., *Core of the Yoga Sūtras: The Definitive Guide to the Philosophy of Yoga* (London: Thorsons, 2012), p.15.

14. Suzuki, Shunryū, *Zen Mind, Beginner's Mind: Informal Talks on Zen Meditation and Practice* (Boulder: Shambhala, 2020), p.1.

15. Ibid., p.128.

16. Source: https://www.lionsroar.com/dharma-dictionary-kokoro/ Retrieved September 5, 2023.

17. Source: https://www.yogapedia.com/definition/5678/hridaya-Retrieved September 5, 2023.

18.   Source: https://www.lionsroar.com/dharma-dictionary-kokoro/
       Retrieved September 5, 2023.

19.   From Eihei Dōgen's *Shōbōgenzō* as quoted in Stone, Michael,
       *Awake in the World: Teachings from Yoga and Buddhism for leading an
       engaged life* (Boulder: Shambhala, 2011).

20.   Frydman, Joshua, *The Japanese Myths: A guide to gods, heroes and
       spirits* (London: Thames & Hudson, 2022), p.33.

21.   McKinney, Meredith, (trans.), *Gazing at the Moon: Buddhist poems of
       solitude* (Boulder: Shambhala, 2021), p.89.

22.   Source: https://japannews.yomiuri.co.jp/society/general-
       news/20221109-69706/ Retrieved Sept, 7, 2023.

23.   Deal, William E., *Handbook to Life in Medieval and Early Modern
       Japan* (Oxford: Oxford University Press, 2006), p.40.

24.   Source: https://japannews.yomiuri.co.jp/society/general-
       news/20221109-69706/ Retrieved September 7, 2023.

CHAPTER 4

1.   Find out more at daihonzan-eiheiji.com/en/

2.   Katagiri, Dainin, *Each Moment is The Universe: Zen and the Way of
      Being Time* (Boulder: Shambhala, 2007), p.11.

3.   For an in-depth analysis of *Uji*, or *'Being-Time'*, I highly
      recommend Roberts, Shinshu, *Being-Time: A Practitioner's Guide to
      Dōgen's Shōbōgenzō Uji* (Somerville: Wisdom, 2018) which is the
      book I carried with me to Eiheiji.

4.   Cohen, Jundo, *The Zen Master's Dance: A guide to understanding Dōgen
      and who you are in the Universe* (Somerville: Wisdom, 2020), p.119.

5.   Find out more at hakujukan-eiheiji.jp

6.   The figure 6,400,099,980 moments is given in *Shukke-Kudoku*,
      one fascicle of Dōgen's masterwork *Shōbōgenzō*. There are many
      translations available, but for example it can be found in Nishijima,
      Gudo, and Cross, Chodo, *(trans.) Master Dogen's Shobogenzo Book 4*
      (Tokyo: Windbell, 1999), p.122.

7.   Ibid.

8.   Rovelli, Carlo, (trans. Segre, Erica and Carnell, Simon), *The Order
      of Time* (London: Penguin, 2018), p.92.

9. Nishijima, Gudo, and Cross, Chodo, (trans.), *Master Dogen's Shobogenzo Book 4* (Tokyo: Windbell, 1999), p.122.
10. Roberts, Shinshu, *Being-Time: A Practitioner's Guide to Dōgen's Shōbōgenzō Uji* (Somerville: Wisdom, 2018), p.26.

CHAPTER 5

1. The full untitled poem by Ōtagaki Rengetsu can be found in Maloney, Dennis, (ed.), *Finding the Way Home: Poems of Awakening and Transformation* (Buffalo: White Pine Press, 2010), p.48.
2. Translation my own. The original poem can be found at *Waka no Sekai* ('World of Japanese *waka* poems'), http://575.jpn.org/article/174793884.html Retrieved September 6, 2023.
3. Translation my own. The original poem can be found in Hoffmann, Yoel, *Japanese Death Poems* (Tokyo; Rutland; Vermont | Singapore: Tuttle, 1986), p.146.

CHAPTER 6

1. Find out more at cabillacornwall.com
2. Tanahashi, Kazuaki, (ed.), *Treasury of the True Dharma Eye: Zen Master Dogen's Shobo Genzo* (Boulder: Shambhala, 2010), p.30.
3. Find out more at yamabushido.jp

CHAPTER 7

1. Source: https://tricycle.org/beginners/buddhism/what-are-the-ten-worlds/ Retrieved September 12, 2023.
2. Katagiri, Dainin, *Each Moment is The Universe: Zen and the Way of Being Time* (Boulder: Shambhala, 2007), p.76.

CHAPTER 8

1. *Itte kimasu* is a ritual parting used when leaving the house. It literally means 'I'm going and coming back', but has the sense of 'I'm off now, see you later'.

2. Source: https://www.wakapoetry.net/tag/minamoto-no-yorimasa/
    Retrieved September 15, 2023.

3. This term is found in Dōgen's *Fukanzazengi*, '*Universally
    Recommended Instructions for Meditation*'. There is an excellent
    commentary available on this by Shōhaku Okumura in *Dharma
    Eye Soto Zen Journal*, number 42, (September 2018), p.18.

4. Ōmine, Akira, (trans. Unno, Taitetsu), 'The Genealogy of Sorrow:
    Japanese View of Life and Death', in *The Eastern Buddhist*, Vol. 25
    No. 2 (Autumn 1992), p.29.

CHAPTER 9

1. Rovelli, Carlo, (trans. Segre, Erica, and Carnell, Simon), *The Order
    of Time* (London: Penguin, 2018), p.87.

2. Translation my own. The original poem can be found at *Waka
    no Sekai* ('World of Japanese *waka* poems'), http://575.jpn.org/
    article/174793884.html Retrieved September 6, 2023.

3. Kerr, Alex, *Finding the Heart Sutra: Guided by a Magician, an Art
    Collector and Buddhist Sages from Tibet to Japan* (London: Allen Lane,
    2020), p.41.

4. Nhat Hanh, Thich, *Awakening of the Heart: Essential Buddhist sutras
    and commentaries* (Berkeley: Parallax, 2012), p.411.

5. Ibid.

6. Find out more at nanzenji.or.jp

7. Kempton, Beth, *The Way of the Fearless Writer: Ancient Eastern
    wisdom for a flourishing writing life* (London: Piatkus, 2022), p.221.

8. Kempton, Beth, *Wabi Sabi: Japanese wisdom for a perfectly imperfect life*
    (London: Piatkus, 2018).

9. Yoshino, Genzaburō, *How Do You Live?* (London: Rider, 2023), p.48.

10. This originates from Case 23 of *Mumonkan* (The Gateless Gate).
    A translation by Nyogen Senzaki and Paul Reps can be found
    online at https://en.wikisource.org/wiki/The_Gateless_Gate/
    Do_Not_Think_Good,_Do_Not_Think_Not-Good (Retrieved
    September 20, 2023). This version asks 'When you do not think
    good and when you do not think not-good, what is your true
    self?' Other commentaries word the koan in ways such as 'Show

me your original face' and 'Show me your original face before you were born'.

CHAPTER 10

1. Find out more at matsunagarokkan.com
2. Source: https://www2.deloitte.com/jp/en/pages/about-deloitte/articles/news-releases/nr20220609.html Retrieved Sept 22, 2023.
3. Source: https://www.japantimes.co.jp/news/2022/03/28/national/social-issues/japan-tokigawa-depopulation/ Retrieved Sept 5, 2023.
4. Source: https://www.japantimes.co.jp/podcast/japan-falling-population/ Retrieved Sept 5, 2023.
5. For more details see furusatokaiki.net/
6. I joined a tour run by Teruyuki Kuchū, owner of guesthouse-couture.com/en/
7. Find out more at kyoto.ayabenouhaku.com
8. Find out more at kyoto.ayabenouhaku.com/post/column-en-origin
9. Find out more at koku-kyoto.com
10. Find out more at sougo.tokyo
11. Find out more at en.satoyama-jujo.com
12. Rengeji Temple, situated in the north east of Kyoto, does not have a website at the time of writing but any taxi driver would be able to take you there. Alternatively, you can go to Miyake Hachiman Station (Eizan Electric Railway from Demachiyanagi) and use Google Maps.

CHAPTER 11

1. Find out more at suiden-terrasse.com/en/
2. Find out more at sorai.yamagata-design.com
3. Find out more at tsuruokacity.com/restaurants/naa
4. Suzuki, Shunryū, *Zen Mind, Beginner's Mind: Informal Talks on Zen Meditation and Practice* (Boulder: Shambhala, 2020).

CHAPTER 12

1. Find out more at shorenin.com
2. Translation my own. The original is known as 日常の五心 (*nichijyō no goshin*) 'The five everyday *kokoro* states' in Japanese Buddhism.
3. This was the way a fellow student worded what Dōgen wrote as 'All the universe is an unceasing process, pursuing things and making them the self, pursuing the self and making it things.' which can be found in Waddell, Norman, and Abe, Masao, *The Heart of Dōgen's Shōbōgenzō* (New York: SUNY Press, 2002), p.33.
4. The song is *Jan Juc Moon* by Xavier Rudd, found on the album *Jan Juc Moon* by Xavier Rudd. See xavierrudd.com

ANATOMY OF THE KOKORO

1. Source: Shinmura, Izuru, *Kōjien daigohan* (Tokyo: Iwanami Shoten, 1998) p.950.
2. Source: https://www.oxfordreference.com/display/10.1093/oi/authority.20110803100041699;jsessionid=4F0531ABCA3FBF27EA77167B70862598 Retrieved September 4, 2023.
3. Source: Pilgrim, Richard B., 'Some Aspects of Kokoro in Zeami' in *Monumenta Nipponica*, Vol. 24, No. 4 (Tokyo: Sophia University, 1969), pp. 393–491. Available at: https://www.jstor.org/stable/2383880 Retrieved September 1, 2023.
4. Source: https://www.rep.routledge.com/articles/thematic/kokoro/v-1 Retrieved September 4, 2023.
5. Find out more about Motoori Norinaga and *mono no aware* at https://plato.stanford.edu/entries/japanese-aesthetics/ Retrieved September 1, 2023.

Bibliography

Please note, book titles which include Japanese words are stated as the word appears in the title of the published book, even if this is different to the Hepburn system of romanisation used throughout the main text of *Kokoro*. For example, Dogen instead of Dōgen, where it is offered without the macron in the book title. The same goes for names of publishers and authors.

English-language sources

Aguirre, Anthony, *Cosmological Koans: A Journey to the Heart of Physics* (London: Penguin, 2020)

Aitken, Robert, *The River of Heaven* (Berkeley: Counterpoint, 2011)

Andoh, Elizabeth, *Kansha: Celebrating Japan's Vegan and Vegetarian Traditions* (New York: Ten Speed Press, 2010)

Aoyama, Shundo, *Zen Seeds: 60 Essential Buddhist Teachings on Effort, Gratitude and Happiness* (Boulder: Shambhala, 2019)

Barthes, Roland (trans. Howard, Richard), *Empire of Signs* (New York: Hill and Wang, 1982)

Beardsley, Richard K., Hall, John W., and Ward, Robert E., *Village Japan* (Chicago: University of Chicago Press, 1959)

Bhakt, Ram, *A Seeker's Guide to the Yoga Sutras: Modern Reflections on the Ancient Journey* (Emeryville: Rockridge Press, 2019)

Bird, Winifred, *Eating Wild Japan: Tracking the culture of foraged foods, with a guide to plants and recipes* (Berkeley: Stone Bridge Press, 2021)

Bjornerud, Marcia, *Timefulness: How Thinking Like a Geologist Can Help Save the World* (Princeton: Princeton University Press, 2018)

Blacker, Carmen, *Collected Writings of Carmen Blacker* (Richmond: Japan Library, 2000)

Brown, Azby, *Just Enough: Lessons from Japan for sustainable living, architecture and design* (Berkeley: Stone Bridge Press, 2009)

Brown, Brene, *Atlas of the Heart: Mapping Meaningful Connection and the Language of Human Experience* (London: Vermillion, 2021)

Brûlé, Tyler, (ed.), 'Trailblazers of Regional Japan', in *Monocle*, Issue 129 (Dec 2019/Jan 2020)

Busch, Akiko, *How to Disappear: Notes on Invisibility in a Time of Transparency* (New York: Penguin Press, 2019)

Claudel, Matthew, *Ma: Foundations for the Relationship of Space-Time to Japanese Architecture,* Exhibition Catalogue (New Haven: University of Yale, MA thesis, 2012)

Cohen, Jundo, *The Zen Master's Dance: A guide to understanding Dōgen and who you are in the Universe* (Somerville: Wisdom, 2020)

Couturier, Andy, *The Abundance of Less: Lessons in Simple Living from Rural Japan* (Berkeley: North Atlantic Books, 2017)

Davies, Roger J., *Japanese Culture: The Religious and Philosophical Foundations* (Tokyo; Rutland, Vermont; Singapore: Tuttle, 2016)

Davies, Roger J. and Ikeno, Osamu (eds), *The Japanese Mind: Understanding Contemporary Japanese* (Tokyo; Rutland, Vermont; Singapore: Tuttle, 2002)

Davis, Bret W., (ed.), *The Oxford Handbook of Japanese Philosophy* (Oxford: Oxford University Press, 2020)

Davis, Malcolm B., (ed.), *Insight Guides Japan* (Hong Kong: APA Publications, 1992)

Deal, William E., *Handbook to Life in Medieval and Early Modern Japan* (Oxford: Oxford University Press, 2006)

Donegan, Patricia, *Haiku Mind* (Boulder: Shambhala, 2008)

Ehrlich, Gretel, *Unsolaced: Along The Way to All That Is* (New York: Pantheon, 2021)

Embree, John F., *A Japanese Village: Suye Mura* (London: Kegan Paul, Trench, Trubner & Co., 1946)

Ertl, John Josef, *Revisiting Village Japan* PhD Thesis (California: University of California, Berkeley, 2007)

Fischer, Norman, *Mountains and Rivers Sutra: A weekly practice guide* (Ottowa: Sumeru, 2020)

Foster, Nelson, and Shoemaker, Jack, *The Roaring Stream: A new Zen reader* (New Jersey: The Ecco Press, 1996)

Freiner, Nicole L., *Rice and Agricultural Policies in Japan: The Loss of a Traditional Lifestyle* (Cham: Palgrave Macmillan, 2019)

Frydman, Joshua, *The Japanese Myths: A guide to gods, heroes and spirits* (London: Thames & Hudson, 2022)

Fujii, Mari, *The Enlightened Kitchen* (New York: Kodansha, 2005)

Fukutake, Tadashi, (trans. Dore, R. P.) *Japanese Rural Society* (London: Oxford University Press, 1967)

Gill, Andrea, *Shugendō: Pilgrimage and ritual in a Japanese folk religion* (Tennessee: University of Tennessee academic paper, 2020)

Halifax, Joan, *The Fruitful Darkness: A Journey Through Buddhist Practice and Tribal Wisdom* (New York: Grove Press, 1993)

Halpern, Jack, (ed.), *NTC's New Japanese-English Character Dictionary* (Tokyo: NTC, 1993)

Harding, Christopher, *The Japanese: A History in Twenty Lives* (London: Allen Lane, 2020)

Hass, Robert, *The Essential Haiku* (Northumberland: Bloodaxe, 2013)

Hawking, Stephen, *The Illustrated A Brief History of Time* (London: Bantam Press, 2018)

Hearn, Lafcadio, *Kokoro: Hints and Echoes of Japanese Inner Life* (Vermont: Tuttle, 1972)

Heine, Steven, *Dogen: Japan's Original Zen Teacher* (Boulder: Shambhala, 2021)

Heine, Steven, (ed.) *Dōgen: Textual and Historical Studies* (Oxford: Oxford University Press, 2012)

Hendry, Joy, *Understanding Japanese Society* (London: Routledge, 1987)

Hill, Dennis, *Yoga Sutras: The Means to Liberation* (Bloomington: Trafford, 2015)

Hillman, James, *The Thought of the Heart and the Soul of the World* (Thompson: Spring Publications, 2021)

Hino, Akira, *Kokoro no Katachi: The Image of the Heart* (Tokyo: Self-published, 2013)

Hoffmann, Yoel, *Japanese Death Poems* (Tokyo; Rutland, Vermont; Singapore: Tuttle, 1986)

Imanishi, Kinji, (trans. Asquith, Pamela J., et al.), *A Japanese View of Nature* (Oxon: Routledge, 2002)

Ishige, Naomichi, *The History and Culture of Japanese Food* (Oxon: Routledge, 2011)

Iyengar, B.K.S., *Core of the Yoga Sūtras: The Definitive Guide to the Philosophy of Yoga* (London: Thorsons, 2012)

Johnson, David W., *Watsuji on Nature* (Evanston: Northwestern University Press, 2019)

Kabat-Zinn, Jon, *Wherever You Go, There You Are: Mindfulness meditation for everyday life* (London: Piatkus, 2019)

Katagiri, Dainin, *Each Moment is The Universe: Zen and the Way of Being Time* (Boulder: Shambhala, 2007)

Katagiri, Dainin, *The Light That Shines Through Eternity* (Boulder: Shambhala, 2017)

Kawai, Kanjirō, (trans. Uchida, Yoshiko), *We Do Not Work Alone* (Kyoto: Kawai Kanjiro's House, 2017)

Kawano, Satsuki, Roberts, Glenda S., and Long, Susan Orpett, (eds), *Capturing Contemporary Japan: Differentiation and Uncertainty* (Honolulu: University of Hawai'i Press, 2014)

Keene, Donald, (ed.), *Anthology of Japanese Literature* (New York: Grove, 1955)

Keene, Donald, *Essays in Idleness: The Tsurezuregusa of Kenkō* (New York: Columbia University Press, 1967)

Kempton, Beth, *The Way of the Fearless Writer: Ancient Eastern wisdom for a flourishing writing life* (London: Piatkus, 2022)

Kempton, Beth, *Wabi Sabi: Japanese wisdom for a perfectly imperfect life* (London: Piatkus, 2018)

Kerr, Alex, *Finding the Heart Sutra: Guided by a Magician, an Art Collector and Buddhist Sages from Tibet to Japan* (London: Allen Lane, 2020)

Kim, Hee-Jin, *Eihei Dōgen: Mystical Realist* (Somerville: Wisdom, 2004)

Kishi, Akinobu, *Sei-ki: Life in Resonance* (London: Singing Dragon, 2011)

Koike, Ryunosuke, (trans. Sugita, Eriko), *The Practice of Not Thinking: A Guide to Mindful Living* (London: Penguin, 2021)

Kornfield, Jack, *The Wise Heart: Buddhist Psychology for the West* (London: Ebury, 2008)

Krummel, John W. M., (ed.), *Contemporary Japanese Philosophy: A Reader* (London: Roman & Littlefield, 2019)

Lakoff, George, and Johnson, Mark, *Philosophy in the Flesh: The Embodied Mind and its Challenge to Western Thought* (New York: Basic Books, 1999)

Lee, Cyndi, *Yoga Body, Buddha Mind* (New York: Riverhead, 2004)

Liotta, Salvator-John A., and Belfiore, Matteo, (eds), *Patterns and Layering: Japanese Spacial Culture, Nature and Architecture* (Berlin: Gestalten, 2012)

Maloney, Dennis, (ed.), *Finding the Way Home: Poems of Awakening and Transformation* (Buffalo: White Pine Press, 2010)

Manzenreiter, Wolfram, and Holthus, Barbara, (eds), *Happiness and the Good Life in Japan* (Oxon: Routledge, 2017)

Marinucci, Lorenzo, *Hibiki and nioi. A study of resonance in Japanese aesthetics.* Article available at https://journals.mimesisedizioni.it/index.php/studi-di-estetica/article/view/879

Matsuo, Bashō, (trans. Reichhold, Jane), *Basho: The Complete Haiku* (New York: Kodansha, 2008)

Matsuo, Bashō, (trans. Hamill, Sam), *Narrow Road to the Interior* (Boulder: Shambhala, 2019)

Matsuo, Bashō, (trans. Yuasa, Nobuyuki), *The Narrow Road to the Deep North and Other Travel Sketches* (London: Penguin, 1966)

McCullough, Helen, (trans.), *The Tale of the Heike* (Stanford: Stanford University Press, 1988)

McKinney, Meredith, (trans.), *Kenkō and Chōmei: Essays in Idleness and Hōkōki* (London: Penguin Classics, 2013)

McKinney, Meredith, (trans.), *Gazing at the Moon: Buddhist poems of solitude* (Boulder: Shambhala, 2021)

McKinney, Meredith, (trans.), *Travels with a Writing Brush: Classical Japanese travel writing from The Manyōshū to Bashō* (London: Penguin Classics, 2019)

Mitford, A.B., *Tales of Old Japan: Folklore, Fairy Tales, Ghost Stories and Legends of the Samurai* (New York: Dover, 2005)

Murata, Yoshihiro et al. (Japanese Culinary Academy), *Introduction to Japanese Cuisine: Nature, history and culture* (Tokyo: Shuhari, 2015)

Murayama, Yuzo, (trans. Winters Carpenter, Juliet), *Heritage Culture and Business, Kyoto Style: Craftsmanship in the Creative Economy* (Tokyo: JPIC, 2019)

Nakano, Kōji, (trans. Winters Carpenter, Juliet), *Words To Live By: Japanese Classics for our Time* (Tokyo: Japan Publishing Industry Foundation for Culture, 2018)

Nepo, Mark, *Falling Down and Getting Up: Discovering Your Inner Resilience and Strength* (New York: St Martin's Essentials, 2023)

Nhat Hanh, Thich, *Awakening of the Heart: Essential Buddhist sutras and commentaries* (Berkeley: Parallax, 2012)

Nhat Hanh, Thich, *Interbeing: Fourteen Guidelines for Engaged Buddhism* (Berkeley: Parallax, 1998)

Nhat Hanh, Thich, *The Other Shore* (Berkeley: Palm Leaves Press, 2017)

Nishida, Kitarō, (trans. Abe, Masao, and Ives, Christopher), *An Inquiry into the Good* (New Haven: Yale University Press, 1990)

Nishida, Kitarō, *Intuition and Reflection in Self-Conciousness* (Nagoya: Chisokudō, 2020)

Nishijima, Gudo, and Cross, Chodo, (trans.), *Master Dogen's Shobogenzo Book 4* (Tokyo: Windbell, 1999)

Nonomura, Kaoru, (trans. Winters Carpenter, Juliet), *Eat Sleep Sit: My Year at Japan's Most Rigorous Zen Temple* (Tokyo: Kodansha International, 1996)

Norbeck, Edward, *Country to City: The Urbanisation of a Japanese Hamlet* (Salt Lake City: University of Utah Press, 1978)

Ō no Yasumaro, (trans. Heldt, Gustav), *The Kojiki: An Account of Ancient Matters* (New York: Columbia University Press, 2014)

Ogawa, Tadashi, (trans. Marinucci, Lorenzo), *Phenomenology of Wind and Atmosphere* (Milan: Mimesis International, 2021)

Okumura, Shōhaku, with O'Connor, Tonen, *Ryōkan Interpreted* (Bloomington: Dōgen Institute, 2021)

Okumura, Shōhaku, 'The 7th Chapter of Shobogenzo Ikaka-myoju (One Bright Jewel) Lecture', in *Dharma Eye Soto Zen Journal*, Number 42 (September 2018), p.18.

Okumura, Shōhaku, *The Mountains and Waters Sūtra* (Somerville: Wisdom, 2018)

Ozeki, Ruth, *A Tale for the Time Being* (London: Canongate, 2013)

Parry, Richard Lloyd, *Ghosts of the Tsunami* (London: Vintage, 2013)

Pilgrim, Richard B., 'Some Aspects of Kokoro in Zeami' in *Monumenta Niponica*, Vol. 24, No. 4 (Tokyo: Sophia University, 1969), pp. 393–491

Pipher, Mary, *A Life in Light: Meditations on Impermanence* (New York: Bloomsbury, 2022)

Pye, Michael, *Japanese Buddhist Pilgrimage* (Sheffield: Equinox, 2015)

Rinpoche, Sogyal, *The Tibetan Book of Living and Dying* (London: Rider, 2008)

Ritchie, Malcolm, *Village Japan: Everyday Life in a Rural Japanese Community* (Tokyo; Rutland, Vermont; Singapore: Tuttle, 1999)

Roberts, Shinshu, *Being-Time: A Practitioner's Guide to Dōgen's Shōbōgenzō Uji* (Somerville: Wisdom, 2018)

Röttgen, Uwe, and Zettl, Katharina, *Craftland Japan* (London: Thames & Hudson, 2020)

Rovelli, Carlo, (trans. Segre, Erica, and Carnell, Simon), *The Order of Time* (London: Penguin, 2018)

Saga, Junichi, *Memories of Silk and Straw: A Self-Portrait of Small-Town Japan* (Tokyo: Kodansha, 1987)

Shiffert, Edith, and Sawa, Yūki, *Anthology of Modern Japanese Poetry* (Vermont: Tuttle, 1972)

Shikibu, Murasaki, (trans. Tyler, Royall), *The Tale of Genji Unabridged* (London: Penguin, 2001)

Shirane, Haruo, *Japan and the Culture of the Four Seasons: Nature, literature and the Arts* (New York: Columbia University Press, 2012)

Singleton Hachisu, Nancy, *Food Artisans of Japan* (Melbourne: Hardie Grant, 2019)

Smith, Patrick, 'Inner Japan', in *National Geographic* Vol 186, No. 3, September 1994 edition pp.64–95

Snyder, Gary, *Mountains and Rivers Without End* (Berkeley: Counterpoint, 1996)

Sōhō, Takuan, (trans. Wilson, William Scott), *The Unfettered Mind: Writings from a Zen Master to a Swordsman* (Boulder: Shambhala, 2002)

Sōseki, Natsume, (trans. McKinney, Meredith), *Kokoro* (London: Penguin, 2010)

Stambaugh, Joan, *The Formless Self* (Albany: State of New York
    University Press, 1999)

Stamm, Joan D., *Heaven and Earth are Flowers: Reflections on
    Ikebana and Buddhism* (Somerville: Wisdom, 2010)

Stevens, John, *One Robe, One Bowl: The Zen Poetry of Ryōkan*
    (Boulder: Shambhala, 2006)

Stevens, John, *Rengetsu: Life and poetry of Lotus Moon* (Vermont:
    Echo Point, 2014)

Stone, Michael, *Awake in the World: Teachings from Yoga and
    Buddhism for leading an engaged life* (Boulder: Shambhala,
    2011)

Stevens, John, *Zen Bow, Zen Arrow* (Boulder: Shambhala, 2007)

Stuart, Colin, *Time: 10 Things You Should Know* (London:
    Orion, 2021)

Suzuki, Shunryū, *Zen Mind, Beginner's Mind: Informal Talks on
    Zen Meditation and Practice* (Boulder: Shambhala, 2020)

Tanahashi, Kazuaki, *Moon in a Dewdrop: Writings of Zen Master
    Dōgen* (New York, North Point Press, 1985)

Tanahashi, Kazuaki, *Sky Above, Great Wind: The Life and Poetry
    of Zen Master Ryokan* (Boulder: Shambhala, 2012)

Tanahashi, Kazuaki, (ed.), *Treasury of the True Dharma Eye: Zen
    Master Dogen's Shobo Genzo* (Boulder: Shambhala, 2010)

Tanahashi, Kazuaki, and Levitt, Peter, (eds.) *The Essential
    Dogen: Writings of the Great Zen Master* (Boulder:
    Shambhala, 2013)

Tannier, Kankyo, (trans. Thawley, Alan), *The Gift of Silence:
    Finding Peace in a World Full of Noise* (London: Yellow Kite,
    2018)

Traphagan, John W., *The Practice of Concern: Ritual, Well-Being
    and Aging in Rural Japan* (Durham: Carolina Academic
    Press, 2004)

Trungpa, Chögyam, *The Teacup and The Skullcup: Where Zen and Tantra Meet* (Boston: Shambhala, 2007)

Uchiyama, Kōshō (trans. Wright, Daitsū Tom, and Okumura, Shōhaku), *Deepest Practice, Deepest Wisdom* (Somerville: Wisdom, 2018)

Uchiyama, Kōshō, *How to Cook Your Life: From the Zen Kitchen to Enlightenment* (Boulder: Shambhala, 2005)

Udaka, Michishige, *The Secrets of Noh Masks* (Tokyo, IBC Publishing, 2015)

Van Zyl, Miezan, (ed.), *Simply Quantum Physics* (London: Dorling Kindersley, 2021)

Waddell, Norman, (trans.) *The Essential Teachings of Zen Master Hakuin* (Boulder: Shambhala, 1994)

Waddell, Norman, *Zen Words for the Heart: Hakuin's Commentary on the Heart Sutra* (Boston: Shambhala, 1996)

Waddell, Norman, and Abe, Masao, *The Heart of Dōgen's Shōbōgenzō* (New York: SUNY Press, 2002)

Warner, Brad, *Don't be a Jerk and Other Practical Advice from Dōgen, Japan's Greatest Zen Master* (Novato: New World Library, 2016)

Warner, Brad, *The Other Side of Nothing: The Zen Ethics of Time, Space, and Being* (Novato: New World Library, 2022)

Watanabe, Shōichi, *The Peasant Soul of Japan* (London: Macmillan, 1989)

Wirth, Jason M., *Engaging Dōgen's Zen: The philosophy of practice as awakening* (Somerville: Wisdom, 2016)

Wirth, Jason M., *Mountains, Rivers and the Great Earth: Reading Gary Snyder and Dōgen in an Age of Ecological Crisis* (New York: SUNY Press, 2017)

Yoshino, Genzaburō, *How Do You Live?* (London: Rider, 2023)

Yuasa, Yasuo, (trans. Nagatomo, Shigenori, and Hull, Monte

S.), *The Body, Self-Cultivation and Ki Energy* (Albany: State University of New York Press, 1993)

Zeami, Motokiyo, (trans. Wilson, William Scott), *The Spirit of Noh: A New Translation of the Classic Noh Treatise The Fushikaden* (Boulder: Shambhala, 2006)

Japanese-language sources

Akane, Akiko, *Jissen kokoro no yōga* (Tokyo: KTC Chūō Shuppan, 2014)

Akane, Akiko, *Kokoro no yōga* (Tokyo: KTC Chūō Shuppan, 2008)

Arai, Man, *Ryōkansan no aigo* (Niigata: Kōkodō, 2008)

Arikawa, Mayumi, *Nichijyō o, kokochi yoku* (Tokyo: PHP, 2012)

Chikushi, Tetsuya, *Surō raifu* (Tokyo: Iwanami, 2006)

Ichida, Noriko, *Jinsei kōhan, jyōzu ni kudaru* (Tokyo: Shōgakukan, 2022)

Inamori, Kazuo, *Kokoro: Jinsei o i no mama ni suru chikara* (Tokyo: Sunmark Shuppan, 2019)

Inata, Miori, *Dewa Sanzan* (Yamagata: Dewa Sanzan Jinjya, 2019)

Iwahana, Michiaki, *Dewa Sanzan* (Tokyo: Iwanami Shinsho, 2017)

Hinohara, Shigeaki, *Tabete naosu fusegu igaku jiten* (Tokyo: Kodansha, 2002)

Hiroi, Yoshinori, *Mu to ishiki no jinruishi* (Tokyo: Tōyō Keizai, 2021)

Hoshino, Fumihiro, *Kanjiru mama ni ikinasai* (Tokyo: Sakurasha, 2017)

Jingukan (ed.), *Kurashi no shikitari jyūnikagetsu* (Tokyo: Jingukan, 2014)

Kage, Kōji, *Kokoro ga wakaru to mono ga ureru* (Tokyo: Nikkei BP, 2021)

Kageyama, Tomoaki, *Yukkuri, isoge* (Tokyo: Daiwa Shobō, 2015)

Kaneko, Yukiko, *Gojyūdai kara yaritai koto, yameta koto* (Tokyo: Seishun Shuppansha, 2019)

Kano, Takamitsu, *Shin shoku dō gen* (Tokyo: Gentōsha MC, 2022)

Kasami, Kazuo, *Inaka o tsukuru* (Tokyo: Commons, 2018)

Kataoka, Tsurutarō, *Kokoro no naka ni sei o motsu* (Tokyo: Sunmark, 2018)

Kawai, Toshio, *Shinri ryōhōka ga mita nihon no kokoro* (Kyoto: Minerva Shobō, 2020)

Koike, Ryūnosuke, *Ima, shindemo ī yō ni* (Tokyo: Gentōsha, 2017)

Kurose, Kikuko, *Kokoro ni naru oto* (Tokyo: Bungeisha, 2022)

Masuda, Miri, *Kokoro ga hodokeru chiisana tabi* (Tokyo: Gentōsha, 2016)

Masuno, Shunmyō, *Zen no kokoro de taisetsu na hito o miokuru* (Tokyo, Kōbunsha, 2023)

Matsuba, Tomi, *Gungendō no ne no aru kurashi* (Tokyo: Ie no hikari kyōkai, 2009)

Matsuba, Tomi, *Mainichi o tanoshimu sutenai kurashi* (Tokyo: Ie no hikari kyōkai, 2016)

Matsuo, Bashō, *Oku no hosomichi* (Tokyo: Kadokawa, 2003)

Matsuo, Bashō, *Bashō zen kushū* (Tokyo: Kadokawa, 2010)

Mizuno, Yaoko, (trans.) *Dōgen Zenji zenshū – Shōbōgenzō 3* (Tokyo: Shunjyūsha, 2022)

Morigami, Shōyō, *Wabi sabi yūgen no kokoro: Seiyō tetsugaku o koeru jyōi ishiki* (Tōkyō: Sakuranohana Shuppan, 2015)

Morishita, Noriko, *Kōjitsu nikki* (Tokyo: Parco Shuppan, 2018)

Murata, Wajyu, *Watashi o ikiru* (Tokyo: Tabata Shoten, 2019)

Nakata, Hidetoshi, *Nihonmono* (Tokyo: Kadokawa, 2018)

Nakano, Tōzen, *Ryōkan* (Tokyo: Sōgensha, 2010)

Nonomura, Kaoru, *Kū neru suwaru: Eiheiji shūgyōki* (Tokyo: Shinchōsha, 1996)

Oki, Sachiko, *Gojyū sugitara, mono wa hikizan, kokoro wa tashizan* (Tokyo: Shuudensha, 2013)

Oki, Sachiko, *Jinsei o yutaka ni suru chiisa na ippun no shuukan* (Tokyo: Shufu to seikatsusha, 2015)

Ōtani, Tetsuo, *Dōgen* (Tokyo: Sōgensha, 2010)

Satchidananda, Sri Swami, (trans. Itō, Hisako), *Integuraru Yōga* (Tokyo: Merukumāru, 2012)

Sen, Genshitsu, *Nihon no kokoro, tsutaemasu* (Tōkyō: Gentōsha, 2016)

Setouchi, Jakuchō, *Hohoemigatari* (Tokyo: Asahi Shinbun Shuppan, 2022)

Shinmura, Izuru, *Kōjien daigohan* (Tokyo: Iwanami Shoten, 1998)

Shinoda, Tōkō, *Hyaku san sai ni natte wakatta koto* (Tokyo: Gentōsha, 2017)

Shiomi, Naoki, *Shiomi Naoki no Kyōto hatsu konseputo hachijyū hachi* (Kyoto: Kyoto Shinbun Shuppan Sentaa, 2023)

Suga, Atsuko, *Kokoro no tabi* (Tokyo: Haruki Bunko, 2018)

Suzuki, Setsuko, (ed.), *Nihon jiten* (Tokyo: Kōdansha, 1998)

Suzuki, Shunryū, (trans. Fujita Isshō), *Zen maindo, bigināzu maindo* (Tokyo: PHP, 2022)

Takahashi, Ayumu, *Adobenchā raifu* (Tokyo: A-Works, 2003)

Tanikawa, Shuntarō, *Shiawase ni tsuite* (Tokyo: Nanarokusha, 2022)

Toshimori, Yūko, *Yūkosanchi no tezukuri kurashi* (Tokyo: Overlap, 2018)

Tsubata, Hideko, and Tsubata, Shūichi, *Kikigatari toki o tameru kurashi* (Tokyo: Shizenshoku Shūshinsha, 2012)

Tsuda, Harumi, *Guddo rukkingu raifu* (Tokyo: Toto Shuppan, 2001)

Tsuji, Shinichi, *Surō raifu hyaku no kīwādo* (Tokyo: Kōbundō, 2003)

Tsuji, Shinichi, *Yukkuri de īn da yo* (Tokyo: Chikuma Purimā, 2006)

Uchida, Ayano, *Shiawase na kokoromochi* (Tokyo: Shufu to seikatsusha, 2022)

Usui, Yuki, *Kokoro ga tsūjiru hitokoto soeru tsūjiru* (Tokyo, Asa Publishing, 2015)

Watamoto, Akira, *Yoga o tanoshimu kyōkasho* (Tokyo: Natsume Shuppan, 2022)

Watanabe, Kaoru, *Chokkan no migakikata* (Tokyo: Gentōsha, 2019)

Yamada, Tsuyoshi, *Byōki, fuchō shirazu no karada ni nareru furusato mura no shokuyō gohan* (Tokyo: Discover 21, 2021)

Yanagisawa, Konomi, *Kore kara no kurashi keikaku* (Tokyo: Daiwa Shobō, 2022)

Yokota, Mayuko, *Hontō ni hitsuyō wa koto ha subete hitori no jikan ga oshiete kureru* (Tokyo: CrossMedia Publishing, 2019)

Yoshizawa Hisako, *Hyakusai no hyaku no chie* (Tokyo: Chūōkōron Shinsha Inc, 2018)

Yuki, Anna, *Jibun o itawaru kurashigoto* (Tokyo: Shufu to seikatsusha, 2017)

Resources

Tips for slow travel in Japan

If this book has inspired you to visit Japan, I am so glad! It is a really wonderful place to spend time. Here are a few thoughts to help you prepare. My personal opinion is that the best way to travel in Japan is to go slowly – to spend a few days in each place rather than rush from here to there packing in a long list of famous sights. If possible, try to get out of the big cities to explore the countryside.

These days most of the 'must see' sights are completely over-crowded, which is not a good experience for anyone, and in some cases is actually damaging to the places themselves and disruptive to the everyday lives of locals. Be different – ask a taxi driver for their favourite quiet place and let serendipity lead the way. Slow down, sit awhile in a garden, take a walk with no particular destination in mind, strike up a conversation with a store owner, or ask for local recommendations. Focus on experiences rather than a checklist of places and you will have a memorable trip.

For my up-to-date personal recommendations of places to go

and things to do and see, be sure to subscribe to my Substack at
bethkempton.substack.com.

How to travel in Japan

- Go with an open mind and open heart.
- Learn a few words of Japanese before you go – even a single greeting goes a long way, and recognising a few simple characters can give you confidence.
- Practise using chopsticks.
- Respect local customs: remove your shoes before going indoors, don't blow your nose in public, don't drop litter, don't tip, don't eat in the street.
- If you take a bath in a public *sento* or *onsen*, wash *before* you get in the bath.
- Talk to local people whenever you can.
- Take small gifts in case you have the chance to visit someone's home.
- Generally, Japan is a quiet place. Keep the noise down, especially in temples, shrines and gardens.
- Smile, you're having an adventure!

Tips on planning

It can be tempting to just go to the places you have heard of, but much magic and mystery lie off the beaten track. If you aren't sure where to start planning your journey, try picking a theme and go from there. Here are a few ideas:

Start with coffee

Japan has a thriving coffee culture, and coffee shops are often at the heart of a strong community in rural areas. You can find coffee shops everywhere – in rice fields, by the ocean, in airstreams, in old bath houses. Instagram is a good place to start. You could find one you'd love to visit then build your trip around that. It will probably take you somewhere you would not otherwise have gone.

Start with an *onsen*

There are thousands of *onsen* (hot springs) all over Japan, many of them in remote towns and villages, some on mountainsides, others by the ocean. All offer an authentic experience of Japanese life, a delight for your body and a soothing experience for your mind. You'll also likely experience warm hospitality and amazing food. *Ryokan* are a wonderful indulgence if your budget can accommodate it. Otherwise, try staying in a local inn (*minshuku*) or Airbnb and just go to the hot spring as a day visitor, often for just a few hundred yen. To begin your search, type 'onsen', plus the area of Japan you'd like to visit, into Google, click on images and take it from there.

Go for the food

Every prefecture, city and town in Japan is famous for something, very often a particular kind of food. Going on a foodie tour of the country can be a wonderful way to explore outside the regular routes, and discover all sorts of culinary delights. Why not challenge yourself to find the best *ramen*, or to sample some particular type of mountain vegetable?

Discover traditional crafts

Go in search of a craft you are interested in. Some of the best potteries in the country are located in beautiful rural towns and villages and can make a great base for hiking or otherwise enjoying the countryside.

Do a farm stay

Many farmhouses have begun opening their doors to visitors, and this can be a great way to meet locals, and explore somewhere away from the usual tourist route. It can be a wonderful experience for children too.

Go skiing/snowboarding

Japan also has some of the best skiing in the world, with slopes that are often much emptier than their European counterparts. Plus, they serve Japanese curry on the slopes, and offer hot springs and snow festivals. Try Nagano, Hokkaidō or Zaō (between Yamagata and Sendai).

Rent a house

Staying in a traditional house, or doing a homestay with a family, can be a wonderful experience. Instead of rushing from place to place, consider staying for a while in one place, getting to know the local area and imagining yourself living there.

Have a magical mystery tour

Get yourself a JR Pass before you go (for great value rail travel), then close your eyes, put your finger on the map and go there. See what you find!

Useful websites

japan.travel website of the Japan National Tourism
    Organization
nihonmono.jp/en/ for ideas on rural places to visit to
    encounter authentic craftsmanship
spoon-tamago.com for the latest on Japanese art, design
    and culture

rome2rio.com for planning journeys between any two
place

willerexpress.com/en/ for cheap long distance buses

japan-experience.com for lovely Japanese homes to rent

jetprogramme.org for the Japan Exchange and Teaching
Programme, if you fancy a career break or a
new challenge

gaijinpot.com for information on living, studying and
working in Japan

thetokyochapter.com for advice on travelling in Japan
with children

deepkyoto.com for excellent travel advice for Kyoto

audleytravel.com/japan for Duncan Flett, one of the best
Japan travel guides I know

tofugu.com for learning Japanese

www.japantimes.co.jp / mainichi.jp/english / japantoday.com
for daily news

Useful apps

Japan Travel by Navitime

Yurekuru for early notification about earthquakes
and tsunamis

Tokyo Metro

Google Maps

Google Translate

Yomiwa

Ecbo Cloak for luggage storage nationwide

WayGo menu translation

XE Currency Converter

72 Seasons

Guidebooks

Japan by Ebony Bizys/Hello Sandwich (Hardie Grant)
Japan by Steve Wide and Michelle Mackintosh (Plum)
Lonely Planet Japan (Lonely Planet)
Mindfulness Travel Japan by Steve Wide and Michelle
　Mackintosh (Quadrille)

To read before you go

A Single Rose by Muriel Barbery (Gallic)
Autumn Light: Japan's season of fire and farewells by Pico Iyer
　(Bloomsbury)
Eat Sleep Sit: My year at Japan's most rigorous Zen temple by
　Kaoru Nonomura (Kodansha)
In Praise of Shadows by Junichirō Tanizaki (Vintage)
Kyoto: The forest within the gate by Edith Shiffert, with Marc
　P. Keane, Diane Durston, Yoshifumi Takeda, and John
　Einarsen (White Pine Press)
Lost Japan: Last glimpse of beautiful Japan by Alex
　Kerr (Penguin)
Memoirs of a Geisha by Arthur Golden (Vintage)
One Robe, One Bowl by John Stevens (Weatherhill)
The Narrow Road to the Deep North and Other Travel Sketches
　by Matsuo Bashō (Penguin Classics)
Travels with a Writing Brush by Meredith McKinney
　(Penguin Classics)
The Bells of Old Tokyo: Travels in Japanese time by Anna
　Sherman (Picador)
Wabi Sabi: Japanese wisdom for a perfectly imperfect life by Beth
　Kempton (Piatkus)

Grief resources

Websites
Optionb.org
Thegoodgrieftrust.org
Macmillan.org.uk
Cruse.org.uk
Mind.org.uk

Podcasts
Griefcast with Cariad Lloyd
Everything Happens with Kate Bowler

Books
The Red of My Blood by Clover Stroud (Doubleday)
The Year of Magical Thinking by Joan Didion (Harper Perennial)
Notes on Grief by Chimamanda Ngozi Adichie
    (Fourth Estate)
A Grief Observed by C.S. Lewis (Faber & Faber)
Softening Time: Collected Poems by Elena Brower
    (Andrews McMeel)
Loss by Donna Ashworth (Black & White)
The Phonebox at the Edge of the World by Laura Imai Messina
    (Manilla Press)

Acknowledgements

When Mr K and I got married, we included a five-yen coin in each of the wedding favours. We got engaged in Japan, so it was a special place for us. In Japanese, 'five yen' is *goen*, which is also a homonym for the word *goen,* meaning the blessing of a serendipitous, treasured relationship that honours the way our lives are mysteriously and beautifully entangled. Certain encounters shift the trajectory of our lives, or leave traces which we revisit over and over through the years. *Kokoro* is built on a web of such connections.

One of the huge joys of writing this book has been my extensive travel in Japan over the past five years. I will for ever be indebted to everyone who allowed me to share my encounter with them in this book, as well as to those who supported my research behind the scenes with introductions, advice and stories of their own. Those people include Shinichirō Ashino, Yukako Sasaki, Kōji Sasaki, Bruce Hamana, Duncan Flett, Daisuke Sanada, Ai Matsuyama, Kao Sōsa, Nele Duprix, Norifumi Fujita, Keiichi Ōmae, Michael Chan, Noriko Hara, Kyōko Adachi, Michiyuki Adachi, Hiroko Tayama, Reishi Tayama, Tina Sakuragi, Kazuo Kasami, Morihisa Akasaki, Misako Akasaki, Teruyuki Kuchū, Asato Nakamura, Hiroshi Noboru, Yūko Nakaji, Mitsuhiro

Watanabe, David Joiner, James Nicol, Chifumi Watanabe, Hatsumi Hiroe, Akiko Koga, Yūko Shōji and Kazumi Masuda.

Deep thanks go to Master Fumio Hoshino and Master Kazuhiro Hayasaka for opening the Dewa Sanzan mountains for me, and to Takeharu Katō *and team* for facilitating my trips, *yamabushi* training and interviews. I will always be grateful to Yamagata itself, a place that welcomed my older brother and me a quarter of a century ago, and gave us a home and a network of some of the warmest, kindest people I have ever known, as well as mountains, snow and incredible food.

I am immensely grateful to a number of people whose dedication, rigour and specialist scholarship helped me to explore ideas from many centuries ago. Those people include Shinshu Roberts, Dainin Katagiri, Peter Levitt, Kazuaki Tanahashi, Norman Waddell, Masao Abe, Hee-Jin Kim, Jane Reichhold, Sam Hamill, Nobuyuki Yuasa, Shōhaku Okumura, Meredith McKinney, Juliet Winters Carpenter, Carmen Blacker, Donald Keene, Jundo Cohen, John Stevens, Brad Warner and Steven Heine.

The epilogue of *Kokoro* is an homage to two fantastic books that taught me so much about Dōgen, namely *Each Moment is the Universe: Zen and the Way of Being Time* by Dainin Katagiri, and *Moon in a Dewdrop: Writings of Zen Master Dōgen* edited by Kazuaki Tanahashi.

I would also like to offer my gratitude to the helpful staff at the Kanji Museum (Kyoto), the Furusato Kaiki Shien Sentā (Tokyo), the Bodleian Japanese Library (University of Oxford) and at Eiheiji, Hakujukan, Matsunaga Rokkan, Satoyama Jūjō, Zenbō Seinei, Higashi Honganji, Rengeji and Shōrenin.

I am also incredibly grateful to Professor Yoshinori Hiroi of the University of Kyoto for the wonderful foreword for this book, and the many hours of conversation that let to it.

Over the past five years, and particularly during this most recent year, I have received incredible support from so many people, in real life and in my online community. You know who you are. Please know I am so grateful.

Writing books takes time, and I am indebted to the people whose generosity and hard work made it possible for me to focus on this project whenever I needed to: Lilla Rogers, Becky McCarthy, Louise Gale, Jennie Stevenson, Rachael Taylor, Vic Dickenson, Kelly Crossley, Simon Brown, Rachael Hibbert, Mark Burgess and Liam Frost.

My books would not exist in the world without the work of my beloved agent Caroline Hardman, Hana Murrell and the team at Hardman & Swainson, or Jillian Young, Jillian Stewart and the team at Piatkus and Little, Brown. Thank you all so much. It is a joy to work with you. Many thanks also to Matt Burne for the beautiful cover for *Kokoro*, which features Gassan under a full moon.

I am so grateful to Seiko Mabuchi and Audrey Flett for support in checking Japanese language and cultural references and historical facts, and for companionship through the final weeks of writing. Any errors that have slipped through the net are my responsibility.

Thank you to Rachel Kempton for being my early reader, for offering the most thoughtful suggestions and reminding me at the toughest moments that I am living my writerly dream, even when that looks like a tracksuit and a heated-up frozen fish pie from the supermarket.

To Lisa, who gave me your blessing to share about you in this book: thank you for your friendship. You are so deeply missed. May you rest in peace. Actually, may you keep dancing.

To the Giraffes, I will always remember the way you took care of Mum, and of me. Thank you.

To Mr K, Sienna and Maia, you have my heart, always.

To Mum, your death still seems unreal to me. I still go to call you with news, or imagine you getting off the train with your arms stretched wide so the girls can run into them. Your absence has only served to strengthen the lasting imprint of your presence. Thank you for all you are still teaching me.

Side note (true story): as I finished typing this paragraph I looked up and there in the sky behind my desktop was the most enormous, brightest rainbow. Mum, I hope that was you.

Index